EARTH, FIRE AND SEA

The Untold Drama of Creation

EARTH, FIRE AND SEA

The Untold Drama of Creation

R. Russell Bixler

Baldwin Manor Press

EARTH, FIRE AND SEA:
The Untold Drama of Creation
Copyright 1986 by R. Russell Bixler
Published by Baldwin Manor Press
4722 Baptist Road
Pittsburgh, Pennsylvania 15227
All rights reserved
Unless otherwise identified, scripture
quotations in this book are from the
Revised Standard Version
Manuscript typed by Ruth Coles
Typesetting by Jean Stewart
Artwork by Waltraud Hendel
Layout by Helen Mierski
Photo processing by Harry Hendel
Proofreading by Linda Wilson

ISBN   0-9617094-0-5

DEDICATION

 With their reactions ranging from enthusiastic to indignant, many scholars across the nation — even across the sea — have made countless valuable suggestions. Some of their critiques seemed devastating at first glance, repeatedly demanding further research and innumerable revisions. The basic premises however have remained unshaken through all these rigorous examinations. This book is dedicated to each of these special friends.

CONTENTS

FOREWORD BY A SCIENTIST

The doctrine of creation will be a strong stimulus to research, and may become a source of revitalization in the Church of the 21st century. Some scholars predict that the doctrine of creation will become as pivotal for future reformation as was the doctrine of salvation by faith in the 16th century. Therefore this book — which is a treatise on creation — is a harbinger of good things to come in the world of Christian literature and theology.

Furthermore, this work is of outstanding intrinsic merit. It is written with directness, with enthusiasm, with competency and with in-depth quality research. The author has a wide-ranging mind, and he does not hesitate to draw from the wells of thought dug by early Church Fathers, medieval Jewish scholars and contemporary liberal theologians. Notwithstanding, his approach is essentially and clearly conservative. He proceeds from an unswerving commitment to scripture as the Word of God and understands the panorama of Earth history as displaying the works of God. His book will deepen the thought and strengthen the faith of many, including those who may disagree with, or reserve judgment on, his conclusions.

Ex nihilo creation is a long-standing doctrine of the Church in the matter of origins. In their eagerness to exclude evolutionists, several vigorous creationist parachurch organizations have included in their statement of faith this doctrine as a "litmus test" of orthodoxy. Mr. Bixler subjects this doctrine, *ex nihilo* creation, to a rigorous examination and comes up with a most interesting and surprising conclusion.

His historical research is careful and thorough, and he demonstrates an evident competency in dealing with the textual materials in their original languages, Hebrew and Greek. His exegesis of the first verse of Genesis is of particular interest and of crucial importance to his main thesis.

In writing on the doctrine of creation, in depth, the author has taken into account the great texts of Genesis, plus related texts in the Psalms, the Prophets and the New Testament. However, he draws rather sparsely from the Book of Job. One would hope that perhaps a sequel volume will address more thoroughly the great texts in the Book of Job, especially God's speech, chapters 38-41, both for their textual import and for the nature of Job's response to that revelation experience. Nevertheless, the treatise as it stands is an exciting,well-conceived, remarkable work.

Donald W. Patten

Author of *The Biblical Flood and the Ice Epoch* (1966) and *The Long Day of Joshua and Six Other Catastrophes* (1973) with Ron Hatch and Loren Steinhauer; editor of the six-volume *Symposium on Creation*; contributor to *Catastrophism & Ancient History, Creation Research Society Quarterly* and *Kronos*. He is the founder of Microfilm Service Company of Seattle and Portland.

February 1986

FOREWORD BY A BIBLICAL SCHOLAR

In a day when the Bible-science controversy rages more hotly than ever Russell Bixler endeavors to goad evangelical scholars to reconsider biblical creationism. He presents a strongly reasoned case to challenge the traditional exegesis of Gen. 1:1-3, which for 18 centuries has fallen in line with *creatio ex nihilo* — the doctrine that God created the earth out of nothing. The reader finds himself asking whether the allusions to the mythological terms in Job, Psalms and Isaiah are in reference to God's struggle with the forces of chaos at Creation, to the global cleansing of evil in the Deluge, or to Yahweh's victory over the forces of Pharaoh at the Red Sea.

For one who is not a professional scientist, Mr. Bixler evidences widespread knowledge of the various pertinent disciplines. His study is especially valuable in retrieving for us the conclusions of Jewish and Christian teachers ever since the close of the biblical canon. This is no mere academic ax to grind, but the formulation of his devoted research in Bible and science over several decades. He is burdened for truth — God's truth as revealed primarily in scripture but also in nature. Boldly he provokes us to listen again to what the lines of ancient scripture are really proclaiming as well as to the most recent theories of geology and astronomy.

Let not the admittedly speculative interpretations of various lesser issues deter us from setting aside our pre-conceptions long enough to take another careful look at Creation and the age of the earth.

John Rea, Th.D.
Professor of Old Testament
School of Biblical Studies
CBN University
May 1986

INTRODUCTION

> Curiosity about our beginnings continues to haunt the
> human race. It will not call off the quest for
> its origins.[1]

The ancient Hebrew (as well as all of his contemporaries)
was also deeply concerned about his origins. Of course, he
knew quite well the Drama of his own story; it is we today
who are not certain of our story. Our origins have been
sorely confused by a return to paganism in the name of
Science. Therefore, we moderns must redefine our earliest
genealogy anew.

Scientific creationism is helping us accomplish that quest
by enthusiastically restating our heritage for this generation.
Tragically, a great amount of that effort must be dedicated
toward exposing the massive fallacies of those twin 19th-
century philosophies, uniformitarianism[2] and evolution.[3]

In opposition to these erroneous philosophies, the Bible
presents natural history as catastrophic, and the supporting
historical and geological evidence for catastrophism is
overwhelming. Scientific creationism is beginning to fulfill
its promise in this final quarter of the 20th century.

---

[1] Henri Blocher, *In the Beginning*, trans. David G. Preston,
Downers Grove, Ill: Inter-Varsity Press, 1984, p. 15.

[2] Uniformitarianism: The theory that all geological phenomena
may be explained as resulting from a continuity of currently-
observable processes and rates, such as erosion or vulcanism;
global natural catastrophes in recent times are excluded from
consideration.

[3] Evolution: Generally, the theory that all life is explained
by the initial chance appearance of simple forms of life followed
by increasing organization and complexity through immense
periods of time. A divine Power may or may not be involved; if
so, the word "chance" might be deleted.

Nevertheless, Creation Science is seriously divided within itself. The most controversial issue is the age of the earth. Some creationists, examining the scientific data indicating long ages, have attempted various means of re-interpreting Gen. 1 in order to accommodate the natural evidence for an *old* earth. Other creationists, just as competent in their science, hold to the traditional translation — and literal interpretation — of Gen. 1, pointing to the vast array of valid indicators of a *young* earth.[4]

As a result of the conflict, the growing creation science movement is experiencing difficulty in establishing its credibility.[5] Surprisingly, both sides may be right, and both may be wrong. The many scattered biblical allusions to the Creation may resolve at least a significant area of disagreement when scriptures are studied in context, without prejudice.

The key is 900-year-old Jewish scholarship which provides the primitive interpretation of Gen. 1:1-3. The correct syntax of these verses, more acceptable grammatically than that to which we are accustomed, permits a radically different approach to the question of Earth's age. Coupled with the other catastrophic events portrayed in the Bible *passim*, the original *Hebrew* understanding of creation provides a most satisfying resolution of some of the major biblical and scientific difficulties. Nothing is forced; the exegesis flows naturally when perceived in context. Theology and geology we shall find are more compatible than usually acknowledged.

---

[4] A "creationist" is defined as one who accepts a special, one-time divine creation based upon biblical statements, while denying the theory of organic evolution of life. There is room for disagreement about ages within creationism.

[5] See, e.g., *Christianity Today*, Vol. XXVI, No. 16, October 8, 1982, pp. 22-26.

This research explains — biblically — why some scientific indicators suggest an old earth and other data picture a young earth. God's word is Truth: if "the facts" disagree with the Bible, then there must be something wrong with either our perception of the facts or our perception of the Bible. "It is a frequent dictum in works on Bible and Science for the writer to affirm that the Bible never contradicts 'true' science."[6] This statement was made with a strong note of irony, but I believe it to be true nevertheless. As one reads recent creationist literature, he cannot help being impressed with the quality of some of the serious research being done. Creation scientists usually get their natural facts straight; they are keenly sensitive to erroneous interpretation of those data. Their weaknesses lie more often in either improper biblical exegesis or religious prejudice. The exegesis and the prejudice are the main concerns of this treatise.

The earth is both old and young!

Consider carefully this seeming paradox as we journey through an investigation together. Scriptural exegesis is discussed only in terms which can be understood by the intelligent, non-Hebrew-reading student. Reference is made to the commentators for technical aspects whenever appropriate.

Questions and objections will arise in the reader's mind during a study of this book. It is urged that final judgments not be made until after reading the section entitled "Questions." Presumably all reasonable objections will be answered satisfactorily there.

Many knowledgeable friends have read the manuscript and have made helpful criticisms. I have seriously considered their every comment, incorporating some and rejecting

---

6 Bernard Ramm, *The Christian View of Science and Scripture*, Grand Rapids: Eerdmans, 1955, p. 42.

others, all the while stubbornly refusing to yield ground in controversial areas where I felt the weight of evidence upheld my positions.

All biblical and apocryphal references are, unless otherwise noted, from the Revised Standard Version. The questions of authorship and dating of the composition of Gen. 1 are avoided. This study is not an attempt to interpret a "basic message" of Gen. 1, but only to work with the scriptural materials as they impinge upon the subject of creation science. The greater emphasis is upon the age of *inorganic* earth rather than life upon the earth.

PREFACE

I am a creationist. I accept a quite literalistic view of Gen. 1, affirming the belief that God did indeed create the heavens and the earth in six actual "earth days."

Creation science today requires its students to be polymaths, with interdisciplinary interests. I come to this subject as a student of the Bible with an interest in the philosophy of science, writing as a non-specialist, a non-scientist, for heuristic purposes, asking the specialists to pursue the subjects further. I apologize in advance for being incompetent to remove all vestiges of inconsistency.

I also write to Christians. This book is not an attempt to convince anyone of the truths of scientific creationism. Rather, it assumes that the reader is already convinced. The reader will notice that I am eclectic, choosing materials selectively — but always in proper context — from writers who might disagree sharply with my conclusions. Some sources are modern, some older and some ancient. Christians should not fear truth wherever it may be found.

Most of the good biblical scholarship of the past hundred years has been accomplished by "liberal" Bible scholars. In the midst of their writings, however, are often found serious errors, usually indicating overemphasis on post-Enlightenment rationalistic logic. The "conservatives" (with whom I tend to identify), on the other hand, seem to be limited by certain religious doctrines which may or may not be scriptural. So I have tried to remain alert constantly to intrusions of non-scriptural, pious assumptions, to modern myths and half-truths, and to rationalistic world views, yet always sensitive to biblical truth. The best of both worlds — liberal and conservative — has provided a most delightful study.

Many liberal Bible commentators would tend to agree with the exegesis contained herein. Those same scholars, however, would call "myth" that which I accept as historical fact dressed in ancient cultural clothing. Liberals are uncritically committed to a uniformitarian, evolutionary world view. Thus they normally think of these most ancient biblical narratives as mythological. Liberal commentators will not — indeed, cannot — apply the same critical tools to their uniformitarian world view that they apply to the scriptures. Although being deeply appreciative of the early narratives of Genesis, they perceive these verses as ancient (meaning, primitive) man's less-than-adequate understanding of physical reality. Liberal scholars are simply unable to grasp what creationists are about as they delve into the scriptures; such a work as this present one would be received with disdain. Creationism is pejoratively labelled "anti-science."

At any rate, liberal Bible scholarship contributes, not purposefully, but unwittingly, to a better understanding of the Old Testament for creationists. The *caveat* is to recognize the diamonds among the cut glass. Von Rad states the liberal view well.

> Without doubt, there is to be found here [in Gen. 1] a great deal of the knowledge of the origin of the world that had been worked out and taught at the time, and as knowledge it is largely obsolete today.[1]

Liberal commentators, with such assumptions, are offended by attempts to reconcile Genesis and modern scientific discoveries.

> It is a naive and futile exercise to attempt to reconcile the biblical accounts of creation with the findings of modern science. Any correspondence which can be discovered or ingeniously established between the two

---

[1] Gerhard von Rad, *Genesis*, Philadelphia: Westminster, 1961, p. 48.

must surely be nothing more than mere coincidence.[2] The liberal point of view was the same a century ago: "To seek for even a kernel of historical fact in such cosmogonies is inconsistent with a scientific point of view."[3]

How ironic that many modern scholars are so eager to demythologize Genesis, yet are quite unwilling to subject uniformitarianism and evolution to the same process of falsification! So great a scholar as William F. Albright would have disagreed sharply with contemporary liberal writers regarding Gen. 1: "In fact, modern scientific cosmogonies show such a disconcerting tendency to be short-lived that it may be seriously doubted whether science has yet caught up with the Biblical story."[4] We who have such great respect for truth must not allow ourselves to be intimidated by changeable human sciences!

Tradition, on the other hand, also limits sound biblical interpretation. Wagner wonders anxiously "...if being a Christian means knowing in advance what the Bible will say."[5] Westerman adds, "We have some extremely deeply rooted notions regarding the creation of the world and of man which...do not come from the text of the Bible, but

---

[2] Nahum M. Sarna, *Understanding Genesis*, N.Y.: McGraw-Hill, 1966, pp. 2, 3.

[3] Heinrich Zimmern and T.K. Cheyne, art. "Creation," *Encyclopaedia Biblica*, Vol. I, ed. T.K. Cheyne and J. Sutherland Black, N.Y.: Macmillan, 1899, p. 938. Cf. Conrad Hyers, *The Meaning of Creation*, Atlanta: John Knox Press, 1964, esp. chap. 1.

[4] W. F. Albright, "The Old Testament and Archaeology," *Old Testament Commentary*, ed. Herbert C. Alleman and Elmer E. Flack, Philadelphia: Muhlenberg Press, 1948, p. 135.

[5] Claus Westermann, *The Genesis Accounts of Creation*, trans. Norman E. Wagner, Philadelphia: Fortress Press, 1964, p. iv.

from the history of its interpretation."[6] It is strongly urged
that the reader remember Westermann's words throughout
this study.   The fideism of American fundamentalism is
commendable; it is largely responsible for the exciting
explosion of scientific creationism in our generation.   But
fideism to this author is insufficient; faith must also vindicate
itself in actual experience.   Our faith should stand upon the
Bible and doctrines properly derived from its study, but we
ought to expect God to authenticate those scriptures in
today's world.   True biblical faith is far more than blind.
We should also challenge doctrines whose roots are found in
improper exegesis or in the interaction of the Church and
human culture.   American fundamentalism needs to reassess
some of its tenets, discarding that which is a mere product
of post-Enlightenment thinking.

I make two points.   First, I reject any attenuation of
scripture: compromising God's word in order to accommodate Man's word produces erroneous results.   Second, I
reject religious prejudice, such as the forcing of a 19th century
faith upon the Bible.   The Bible should be allowed to speak
for itself, on its own terms.   As Eichrodt says,

> In deciding...on our procedure for the treatment of
> OT thought, we must avoid all schemes which derive
> from Christian dogmatics....Instead, we must plot our
> course as best we can along the lines of the OT's
> own dialect.[7]

That word of wisdom will guide us throughout this book.

---

[6] *Ibid.*, p. 1.   Cf. Ramm, *op. cit.*, pp. 40-42.

[7] Walther Eichrodt, *Theology of the Old Testament*, Philadelphia:
Westminster, 1967, p. 33.

I THE DEBATE AMONG CREATION SCIENTISTS

The King James Version of the Old Testament is based on very late manuscripts of the Hebrew (Masoretic) text. It provides a chronology from which the 17th-century bishop, James Ussher, calculated a "creation" date of 4004 B.C. Other students have arrived at variant dates, all of which are within a few hundred years of Ussher's.[1] The Samaritan Torah however, dating from some time after the final break with the Jews in the 5th century B.C., provides a somewhat longer chronology, and the 3rd century B.C. Greek Septuagint allows for a yet more extended chronology.[2] However, all three textual traditions agree on one fact: the date of the Creation described in Genesis 1 and 2 can be placed no more than a few thousand years ago. Certainly proposals of millions or billions of years fly in the face of the biblical testimony.

Yet scientists who are Christians are divided sharply on the basis of the available scientific data.[3] Some seem to be "fudging" the natural evidence; those who disagree seem to be "fudging'" the biblical evidence.

---

[1] Ussher had many predecessors: see Andrew D. White, *A History of the Warfare of Science with Theology in Christendom*, Vol. I, N.Y.: D. Appleton & Co., 1898, pp. 249f.

[2] Sir Walter Raleigh, in his *History of the World* (1603-16), chose the Septuagint for his chronology because it provided an older and (to him) seemingly more reasonable date for creation. *Ibid.*, p. 254.

[3] A recent Bible conference scheduled two competent creation scientists (among other speakers), one proposing a "young" earth and the other just as firmly contending for an "old" earth.

The scientific data do appear to be contradictory. Published radiometric dates, for example, put the earth's age at billions of years. Old Earth supporters often accept uncritically most of these dates as reasonably accurate. However, competent challengers have called into question some of the basic assumptions of radiometric dating: long ages are *assumed*; original conditions are *assumed*; conditions through the ages are *assumed*. Measurements have been challenged because of known selectivity in eliminating samples that disagree with predetermined dates.[4] Radiometric dating is based upon the uniformitarian hypothesis.

The Bible could well be addressing this matter of radiometric dating by the uranium-lead, potassium-argon and rubidium-strontium "yardsticks." Lead is rather volatile, rubidium and, especially, argon are even more volatile; in case of great amounts of heat during the "creation catastrophe," highly-significant amounts of these volatile elements would have been dissipated, immediately contaminating all

---

[4] For a critique of *radiocarbon* dating and the methods of its enthusiasts, see Robert E. Lee (not a creationist), "Radiocarbon: Ages in Error," *Anthropological Journal of Canada*, Vol. 19, No. 3, 1981, pp. 9-29; reprinted in *Creation Research Society Quarterly*, Vol. 19, No. 2, Sept. 1982, pp. 117f. Lee says, with a touch of irony, "Radiocarbon dating has somehow avoided collapse onto its own battered foundation, and now lurches onward with feigned consistency. The implications of pervasive contamination and ancient variations in carbon-14 levels are steadfastly ignored by those who base their argument upon the dates" (*CRSQ*, p. 125).

Physical chemist Melvin A. Cook, author of *Prehistory and Earth Models* (London: Parrish, 1966), said in a letter dated May 5, 1976: "One *must* handle K-A dating, consistent with all the facts dealing with it, by simply dismissing it as unscientific and completely unreliable, indeed absurd. They simply don't publish the sort of facts they know about that would kill K-A dating once and for all if they are known." (Alfred de Grazia, *Homo Schizo I*, Princeton: Metron Publications, 1983, p. 50.)

possible samples for later measurement. Perhaps such severe phenomena were involved in the Creation, the Flood, and/or the events surrounding the Exodus from Egypt. Later the 8th century prophet Isaiah seems to be describing a similar contemporary or imminent catastrophic event in chapter 24.

> Behold, the LORD will lay waste the earth and make it desolate, and he will twist its surface and scatter its inhabitants...The earth shall be utterly laid waste and utterly despoiled; for the LORD has spoken this word. The earth mourns and withers, the world languishes and withers; the heavens languish together with the earth... [T]herefore the inhabitants of the earth are scorched, and few men are left... The city of chaos is broken down... For the windows of heaven are opened, and the foundations of the earth tremble... The earth is utterly broken, the earth is rent asunder, the earth is violently shaken. The earth staggers like a drunken man, it sways like a hut... (Isaiah 24:1, 3,4,6b,10a,18c,19,20a).

Thus even the Bible suggests that age estimates based upon the decay rates of the more volatile elements might be untrustworthy.

A strong candidate for a worldwide *igneous* event — the Flood — is described in Gen. 7:11. The scripture tells vividly how "...all the fountains of the great deep burst forth." Liberal Bible scholars assume that this verse refers to the lowest, watery level of a "three-tiered" universe. However, such exegesis is based upon the pagan, Aristotelian, medieval world view — *not* that of the Old Testament! In practical terms, what else could Gen. 7:11 be portraying but sudden, universal volcanic eruptions on the ocean floor, sending enormous tsunamis (popularly known as tidal waves) hundreds or even thousands of feet high crashing over the land?[5] Would not volatile elements have been dissipated?

---

[5] Cf. Joseph C. Dillow, *The Waters Above*, Chicago: Moody Press, 1981, pp. 267f.

Radiometric dating is generally acknowledged to be greatly affected by vulcanism,[6] sometimes multiplying true ages exponentially, so distorting the results that hundreds of years can appear to be millions. The incredible scope of volcanic activity suggested in Gen. 7:11 would have rendered the totality of Earth's surface utterly contaminated for purposes of radiometric dating. In the light of this treatise however it will be seen that, right or wrong, radiometric dating is less relevant to a study of origins than previously thought.

The rabbinic *Book of Jasher* suggests that earthquakes occurred and volcanoes erupted globally during the Deluge.[7] Ginzberg notes that Jewish traditions insist..."the punishment *by fire* during the flood is connected with the conception of the world conflagration which then took place for the first time."[8] Further, an enormous heat load would have been generated — by the latent heat of condensation (of water vapor), and also by the interaction of the raindrops and the atmosphere.[9] Ginzberg accordingly, quoting other ancient Jewish records, says that God sent scalding rain during those 40 days in order to burn the human race as it struck.[10]

Recent research has revealed what is apparently a global layer of soot at the Cretaceous-Tertiary boundary. Found in samples from Denmark, Spain and New Zealand, the carbon

---

[6] Lee, *op. cit.*, (*CRSQ*), p. 119.

[7] *The Book of Jasher, faithfully translated from the Original Hebrew into English*, Salt Lake City: J. H. Parry & Co., 1887, p. 12. Although written in a rabbinic style, its antiquity has been challenged.

[8] Louis Ginzberg, *The Legends of the Jews*, Vol. I, Philadelphia: The Jewish Publication Society of America, 1947, p. 178.

[9] Dillow, *op. cit.*, p. 271.

[10] Ginzberg, *op. cit.*, Vol. V, p. 159.

is quantitatively equal to that of 10% of the earth's present biomass, indicating the enormity of the fires. Previous hypotheses of a cometary or meteoritic encounter seem to be ruled out by these finds, in that such a limited impact could hardly ignite global fires of this magnitude. Further, the expected meteoritic noble gases were not present in the tested samples.[11]

> Tropical rain forests with a large annual rainfall are usually considered unlikely to suffer destruction by forest fire. However, a large percentage of soil cores taken in the Amazon Basin in Venezuela show charcoal layers. Human occupation of the area is dated back to only 3700 years ago, whereas some of the charcoal gives radiocarbon dates up to 6300 years BP. The fires which formed the charcoal cannot therefore have been started by human slash-and-burn cultures...[12]

Thus modern science inadvertently confirms the ancient records of the Deluge. Psalms 18:7-15 is probably reminiscent of this event.

"...All the fountains of the great deep burst forth..." pictures the initiation of the Flood, explaining why relatively immobile marine fossils are generally found at the bottom of Earth's sedimentary strata. The rains followed as dust particles from the global eruptions provided nuclei for raindrops to form. Earthquakes, volcanic eruptions and rains persisted, tearing loose and reshaping massive segments of the earth's surface during seven-and-a-half months. Then "...the fountains of the deep and the windows of the heavens were closed" (Gen. 8:2a). The staggering violence of

---

[11] Wendy S. Wolbach, Roy S. Lewis, Edward Anders, "Cretaceous Extinctions: Evidence for Wildfires and Search for Meteoritic Material," *Science*, Vol. 230, No. 4722, Oct. 11, 1985, pp. 167-70.

[12] *Workshop*, Society for Interdisciplinary Studies, Vol. 6, No. 3, February 1986, p. 26, based on an item in *New Scientist*, January 24, 1985, p. 35.

the continuing ebb and flow had torn up and redeposited sedimentary strata as deep as a mile or more. Coal was at least in part produced by trees and plants that were burning when entombed by the tsunamis. "The evidence strongly supports a process of carbonisation in forest fires, which were extensive, but were checked by flooding before destruction of the forests was complete."[13] Thus may be seen some of the evidences for a young earth and a recent Flood.

On the other hand, proponents of an old earth, beginning with astronomer William Herschel nearly two centuries ago, have been describing the great distances of remote stars, even to billions of light-years. Such a simple proof seems to eliminate the possibility of a youthful universe. Yet many creationists counter by insisting that God created a "mature" world.[14] Adam, for example, was an adult when created, not a helpless baby; the universe likewise, they say, was created fullblown. This "apparent age" or "functioning completeness" theory includes the most distant star — *and* its light! Such a strained argument frustrates old Earth creationists, eliminating immediately another possibility: the dialogue ends right there! Occasional young Earth appeals to Riemannian, curved space impress very few, although Setterfield has proposed an interesting case for a slowly decreasing speed of light.[15]

---

[13] Wilfrid Francis, *Coal: Its Formation and Composition,* 2nd ed., London: Edward Arnold, 1961, p. 625. Cf. John C. Whitcomb, Jr., and Henry M. Morris, *The Genesis Flood*, Grand Rapids: Baker, reprinting 1978, p. 122.

[14] First proposed by Chateaubriand in 1802: Francis C. Haber, *The Age of the World: Moses to Darwin*, Baltimore: The Johns Hopkins Press, 1959, p. 190. Blocher, *op. cit.*, p. 216, credits Philip H. Gosse with the origination of this idea in 1857.

[15] Barry Setterfield, "The Velocity of Light and the Age of the Universe," *Ex Nihilo*, Vol. 4, No. 1, March 1981, and Vol. 5,

While young Earth advocates hurry past those trouble-some stellar distances,[16] they bring up the argument based on Earth's weakening magnetic field, a fact apparently demanding a very limited history.[17] Old Earth proponents counter that paleomagnetic data indicate a weakening magnetic field only during the past two millennia: earlier evidences indicate a strengthening field.[18]

Young Earth enthusiasts appeal to the recent results of Robert Gentry's pioneering research in "pleochroic halos." Studying pre-Cambrian rock, Gentry's work suggests that Earth's basement rock might have been formed instantly, rather than being cooled slowly from magma to rock, as the conventional theory has it. Some creationists have carried Gentry's results to possibly exaggerated conclusions: "The single evidence of the halos is that the basement rocks of the earth were formed suddenly and in a solid state...!"[19] The uniformitarian Establishment responded with scorn to Gentry's published results and, with typical emotional heavyhandedness, made certain that Gentry's research grant was cut off by the National Science Foundation and his "visiting" status was terminated.

No. 3, Jan. 1983. Cf. Paul M. Steidl, "The Velocity of Light and the Age of the Universe," *Creation Research Society Quarterly*, Vol. 19, No. 2, Sept. 1982, pp. 128-31. The present work renders moot the question of the velocity of light.

[16] Cf. David J. Krause, "Astronomical Distances, the Speed of Light, and the Age of the Universe," *Journal of the American Scientific Affiliation*, Vol. 33, No. 4, December 1981, pp. 235-39.

[17] D. Russell Humphreys, "The Creation of the Earth's Magnetic Field," *Creation Research Society Quarterly*, Vol. 20, No. 2, Sept. 1983, pp. 89-94.

[18] Davis A. Young, *Christianity and the Age of the Earth*, Grand Rapids: Zondervan, 1982, pp. 117-124.

[19] William Overn, "The Creator's Signature," *Bible Science Newsletter*, Vol. 20, No. 1, Jan. 1982, pp. 1f.

Obviously, speaking to the question of the age of the earth stirs strong emotional responses. Both sides can muster impressive arrays of evidence. Paradoxically, some of these apparently "proven facts" indicate clearly an *old* earth, and some just as urgently demand a *young* earth.

We must learn to look to the Bible for answers. And, as faithful as ever, God's word unties this Gordian knot. Simply, this work resolves much of the disagreement between the proponents of a young earth vs. those of an old earth. Here is the key.

The contention of this treatise is that the doctrine of creation out of nothing, so dear to many modern Christians, is *not* scriptural!

Based not upon the original Hebrew, but rather upon the earliest Greek translation of Gen. 1, *creatio ex nihilo* began to flower in the 2nd century A.D., and from a heretical — that's right, *heretical* — source at that!

Before responding emotionally to this statement, note carefully all the information presented in this book, and make a decision based upon the biblical and historical evidence. This work proposes a translation of Gen. 1:1-3 somewhat as follows:

> In the beginning of God's creating the heavens and the earth — the earth being a formless waste and darkness being upon the face of the deep and the Spirit of God moving over the face of the waters — God said, "Let there be light!" And there was light.

This translation — remarkably — accounts for the anomalous situation where some natural evidence points toward an *old* earth and some indicates a *young* earth.

That incredible statement will be explained; but first, let's investigate the matter of our "traditional" English translation of Gen. 1:1-3 and how the non-Christian concept of *creatio ex nihilo* came to be orthodoxy.

II THE HISTORY OF OLD TESTAMENT VERSIONS

The *Hebrew* Old Testament as we know it did not receive its final form until well into the Christian era. According to some vague traditions, rabbis meeting about A.D. 90 at Jamnia on the Mediterranean coast of Palestine recognized the canon as being limited to its current 39 books. The 16th century Protestant Reformers later concurred. About A.D. 500 the Jewish Masoretic scribes began to revise and add vowel pointings to the Hebrew Old Testament. The present form of the Hebrew text was completed by these Jewish scholars — but not before the 9th century A.D.! Other than the Dead Sea Scrolls, today we have few portions of the Hebrew Old Testament antedating the Masoretes.

The first *translation* of the Old Testament was begun in the 3rd century B.C. Seventy Jewish scholars, working near Alexandria, Egypt, initiated a translation at the request and expense of King Ptolemy Philadelphus, one of the early successors of Alexander the Great. The project's fulfillment is lost in variant traditions, but the creation narratives — Gen. 1 and 2 — would obviously have been completed early. This Greek translation became the Old Testament of the early Christians, as well as many Diaspora Jews. Even the converted Pharisee, Paul, used the Greek Bible. Although Jerome consulted the Hebrew text liberally for his Latin Vulgate translation from the Greek, it was actually the Protestant Reformers who initiated the return to the Hebrew — away from the Greek — Old Testament by Christians.

The city of Alexandria was thoroughly Greek, the

hellenizing of the Middle East having proceeded rapidly
after the Alexandrian conquest about 330 B.C. Stubborn
resistance to hellenistic culture was found only among
religious Jews (see 1 and 2 Maccabees). Yet noticeable
philosophical changes began to take place in the thinking
of Jewish writers in spite of their Jewishness, especially
those living in the Diaspora. Of importance to our study is
the translation into Greek of Gen. 1:1 by the Seventy (giving
this version the title of "Septuagint," usually symbolized by
"LXX"). The Septuagint states simply in Greek, "In the
beginning God created the heaven and the earth."

This treatise contends that, as can occur in any translation, the LXX rendering of Gen. 1:1 was erroneous.
Actually, the error would be easy to make. Biblical Hebrew
had few vowel sounds until the Masoretes added their "vowel
pointings" a thousand years later, and punctuation was
unheard of. By the 6th century A.D. the original pronun-
ciation and syntax could have become quite difficult to
ascertain. (The original writing of Gen. 1 was more distant
in time from the Masoretic scholars than the one surviving
manuscript of *Beowulf* is from us today, and few modern
Englishmen can understand *Beowulf*!) Improper vocalization of the Hebrew could change the whole sense of a
passage and, in the case of Gen. 1:1, may have contributed
toward just that. Origen's third century transliteration of
the Hebrew Old Testament to Greek (*Hexapla*) indicates that
vocalization had indeed changed significantly before the
Masoretes initiated their prodigious work.[1]

But I suggest that the LXX error in Gen. 1:1 may have
been more deliberate than accidental. The 3rd century B.C.
Jewish translators were quite aware of Greek and Egyptian
polytheistic mythologies. Eager to maintain the distinctive-

---

[1] Cf. Mitchell J. Dahood, *Psalms I*, p. xxii; *Psalms II*, p. xviii,
Anchor Bible, Garden City, NY: Doubleday, 1966.

ness of their God, the scribes might well have made this subtle change in order to eliminate the possibility that other gods could have co-existed with the true God before the Creation. According to *Masseketh Sopherim*, "The Tractate of the Scribes," of the 8th or 9th century A.D., the translators of the LXX later altered a few selected passages of their work for Ptolemy Philadelphus. Gen. 1:1 was specifically noted as one of these emendations.[2] Abraham Geiger, a Jewish scholar of the mid-19th century, suggested that it was for this very reason that Gen. 1:1 was emended by the LXX scribes.[3] However, the variance specifically noted by the Tractate would not significantly alter the meaning of verse 1.[4] Geiger was probably wrong.

Yet there would indeed be good reason for the Jewish translators to alter the intent of the text. At this early period, prior to the Masoretic protectors of "tradition," copyists were not at all averse to adding to and emending scriptures as they copied. How much more so for the translators! Even today translators are tempted to take such liberties.[5] The pagan creation myths were repugnant to the Jewish mind, and by making Gen. 1:1 an independent sentence, the translators may well have felt that they were

---

[2] Henry St. John Thackeray, *The Letter of Aristeas*, London: Society for the Promotion of Christian Knowledge, 1917, Appendix, pp.89f.

[3] Abraham Geiger, *Urschrift und Verbersetzungen der Bibel...*, 1857, pp. 344, 439, 444, noted by John Skinner, *Genesis*, Edinburgh: T. & T. Clark, 1910, p. 14 (footnote); G. J. Spurrell, *Notes on the Hebrew Text of the Book of Genesis*, London: Methuen, 1904, p. 2; August Dillman, *Genesis Critically and Exegetically Expounded*, Edinburgh: T. & T. Clark, 1897, p. 54.

[4] Skinner, *op. cit.*, p. 14 (footnote).

[5] A prominent example is Isaiah 7:14: a "virgin" or a "young woman"?

distinguishing the *real* Creation and the *real* God from the
crude and polytheistic Greek and Egyptian cosmogonies.
Thus it was perhaps that they translated verse 1 as a sentence
complete in itself.

The Septuagint established the model for future translations. The Aramaic Targums were written no earlier than
the 1st century A.D. and the Syriac Peshitta within another
generation-or-two. Both imitated what was by then the
Septuagint "tradition" concerning Gen.1:1.[6] Other translations followed, each of them making the first verse of the
Bible an independent sentence.[7] All early English translations
also followed this now-traditional pattern.[8]

But God has wondrous ways of transmitting and pre-
serving his written word. In the late 11th century the
celebrated Jewish scholar Rashi re-introduced what appears
to have been the original Hebraic interpretation. Rashi
apparently was the first expositor to note explicitly that
proper exegesis should consider the first verse of Genesis
to be a *dependent* clause, with the finite verb "said" in
verse 3 as the main verb of the opening sentence. First
acknowledging that "our rabbis have interpreted it [as the
Septuagint]," Rashi continues,

> But if you should come to interpret it in its plain
> sense,thus explain it: At the beginning of the creation
> of heaven and earth, when the earth was unformed
> and void, and darkness...(etc.), God said, "Let there

---

[6] Cf. Joshua Bloch, "The Influence of the Greek Bible on the
Peshitta," *American Journal of Semitic Languages and Literatures*, XXXVI, Jan. 1920, pp. 161-66.

[7] Skinner, *op. cit.*, pp. 12f. In his *Hexapla* Origen (early 3rd
century) included three Old Testament translations into Greek
(Aquila, Theodotion and Symmachus) in addition to the LXX.

[8] Luther A. Weigle, *The Genesis Octapla*, N.Y.: Thomas Nelson,
1952, pp. 2, 3.

be light."[9]

A generation later the Jewish scholar Ibn Ezra suggested a *third* syntactical arrangement. Ibn Ezra agreed with the temporal quality of verse 1, but disagreed concerning the main verb, which he assumed to be in verse 2, making verse 3 a distinct sentence.

Suddenly, by the 12th century, there were *three* possible translations of Gen. 1:1!

---

[9] Rashi, *The Pentateuch and Rashi's Commentary, Genesis*, ed. Abraham ben Isaiah & Benjamin Sharfman, Brooklyn, N.Y.: S. S. & R. Publishing Co., 1949, p. 1.

In the Beginning...

In the Beginning of...

III EXEGESIS OF GENESIS 1:1-3

Can the syntax of the Hebrew in verse 1 actually permit all three variant translations? Indeed it can, although Ibn Ezra's interpretation appears to contain some weaknesses.

This work will not delve extensively into the technical details of exegesis.[1] One fascinating observation concerning the commentators is that many attempt to demonstrate how one or two of the three possible translations is/are improbable or impossible, thus revealing each one's own preference.

The Hebrew alphabet contains consonants with limited vowel sounds; the proper vocalization was known only to those who spoke it — even as in modern Hebrew. Many

---

[1] Serious students of Hebrew can find such discussions in Franz Delitzsch, *A New Commentary on Genesis*, Edinburgh: T. & T. Clark, 1888, pp. 71f; Skinner, *op. cit.*, pp. 12f; J. M. Powis Smith, "The Syntax and Meaning of Genesis 1:1-3," *American Journal of Semitic Languages and Literatures*, 44, 1928, pp. 108f; Harold G. Stigers, *A Commentary on Genesis*, Grand Rapids: Zondervan, 1976, pp. 47f; E. J. Young, *Studies in Genesis One*, Phillipsburg, N.J.: Presbyterian and Reformed Publishing Co., 1979, pp. 1f; Brevard S. Childs, *Myth and Reality in the Old Testament*, Naperville, IL: Alec R. Allenson, 1960. pp. 30f; von Rad, *op. cit.*, pp. 43f; Weston W. Fields, *Unformed and Unfilled*, Phillipsburg, N.J.: Presbyterian and Reformed Publishing Co., 1978, pp. 149f; E. A. Speiser, *Genesis*, Anchor Bible, Vol. I, Garden City, NY: Doubleday, 1964, pp.3-13; Gerhard F. Hasel, "Recent Translations of Genesis 1:1: a Critical Look," *The Bible Translator*, Vol. 22, No. 4, Oct. 1971, pp. 154-67. Eichrodt, *op. cit.*, Vol. 2, pp. 100f. The most detailed defenses of the traditional (LXX) version are Young, Fields and Hasel; cf. also Eichrodt; Smith and Speiser make cases for Rashi's translation, while Stigers chooses Ibn Ezra's.

centuries after Gen. 1 was written, the Masoretes, in attempting to standardize their scriptures for the ages, added vowel pointings — and only brought confusion to the syntax of verse 1.

> ...The few fragments [of Origen's 3rd century A.D. Greek transliteration of the Hebrew, the Hexapla] that remain...seem to prove...that the present [Masoretic] system of vocalization differs appreciably from the system in use at the time of the composition of the Hexapla...We must still conclude that the mode of reading the text which prevailed when the Hexapla was compiled was not precisely the same as that which is prescribed by the system of vowel points now in use.[2]

The four or five centuries from Origen to the Masoretes obviously made quite a difference.

The Masoretes certainly did not make clear by their pointing how they understood Gen. 1:1. Perhaps they were unsure; more probable is the suggestion that they knew very well how to point verse 1 clearly, but they compromised after a dispute among themselves. Rashi, writing only a few generations later, was the first to try to restore the Hebraic reading to verse 1. During the 19th century — and often since — many biblical commentators seized upon Rashi's proposed syntax, arguing "that this represents the old Jewish tradition."[3] A number of these scholars have been European. Today's translators still seem to be divided all three ways (see Appendix). Representative English versions of Gen. 1:1-3 are given below (all finite verbs in italics):

1) (Traditional) *RSV*: "In the beginning God *created*

---

[2] William Smith & Henry Wace, eds., *A Dictionary of Christian Biography, Literature, Sects and Doctrines*, Vol. III, NY: AMS Press, 1974, pp. 15, 16. However, cf. Peter C. Craigie, *Psalms 1-50* (Word Biblical Commentary, Waco: Word Books, 1983, p. 52), who disagrees, but not convincingly.

[3] Skinner, *op. cit.*, p. 13 (footnote); cf. Hasel, *op. cit.*, p. 157, for a partial listing.

> the heavens and the earth. The earth *was* without form and void, and darkness *was* upon the face of the deep; and the Spirit of God *was moving* over the face of the waters. And God *said*, '*Let* there *be* light'; and there *was* light."

2) (Rashi) *Anchor Bible*: "When God set about to create heaven and earth — the world being then a formless waste, with darkness over the seas and only an awesome wind sweeping over the water — God *said*, '*Let* there *be* light.' And there *was* light."

3) (Ibn Ezra) *An American Translation*: "When God began to create the heavens and the earth, the earth *was* a desolate waste, with darkness covering the abyss and a tempestuous wind raging over the surface of the waters. Then God *said*, '*Let* there *be* light!' and there *was* light."

Note the great variation of main verbs. All three translations are possible in view of the unclear pointing of the Masoretic text.[4]

> [I]t is important that we should not enter into the attempt to translate these verses with preconceived ideas about what it must or must not say. We must allow the writer to speak for himself.[5]

Is Gen. 1:1 an independent sentence, as in the traditional interpretation? If so, the opening word of the Bible, *bereshith* ("In the beginning...") is said grammatically to be in the "absolute" state. Or, is Gen. 1:1 a dependent clause, with the main clause in verse three (or, two)? If so, *bereshith* ("In the beginning of...") is said to be in the "construct" state. The controversy is centered upon the syntactical

---

[4] Cf. Robert Davidson, *Genesis 1-11*, London: Cambridge Univ. Press, 1973, pp. 12-13; Childs, *op. cit.*, p. 31; William F. Albright, "Contributions to Biblical Archaeology and Philology," *Journal of Biblical Literature*, Vol. 43, 1924, p. 364.

[5] W. R. Lane, "The Initiation of Creation," *Vetus Testamentum*, Vol. XIII, 1963, p. 66.

interpretation of *bereshith*, which means, quite literally, "in beginning," or "in beginning of."

First, the missing definite article in the Masoretic text militates against the traditional translation (the absolute state), which usually has the article present, while the second option (the construct state) can never have the article present.[6] There are four extant early Greek transliterations of Gen. 1:1. Hasel says the spellings of two of these four "support the view of Gen. 1:1 as a main clause because apparently some read the definite article and understood the first word to read [*bareshith*][7] (This spelling n the transliteration implies the definite article). Jerome (A.D. 400), however, transliterated the initial word as *bresith*.[8] On the other hand, the ancient Greek transliteration of the Samaritan Torah is *bareshit*, which also implies the definite article.[9] But of course the LXX centuries before had established the tradition for vocalizing the Hebrew of verse 1 for Greek-reading Jews, all of which causes us to wonder about the lack of unanimity among the transliterations. The results, as may be observed, are quite inconclusive.

Bereshith is the combination of *be* (the inseparable preposition "in") and *reshith* ("beginning" or "beginning of"). This combined form as seen in the Masoretic rendering of Gen. 1:1 (*bereshith*) is found elsewhere in the Old Testament only in Jeremiah — 26:1; 27:1; 28:1; 49:34 — and *only* in the

---

6 Fields, *op. cit.*, pp. 152-53.

7 Hasel, *op. cit.*, p. 159; Alexander Heidel, *The Babylonian Genesis*, 2nd ed., Chicago: Univ. of Chicago, p. 93, quoting Fridericus Field, *Origenis Hexaplorum supersunt*, Vol. I,Oxford: 1875, p. 7; cf. Origen, *Hexapla*, in J.-P. Migne, *Patrologiae Graecae*, Vol. XV, pp. 143-44.

8 Heidel, *op. cit.*, p. 93.

9 Hasel, *op. cit.*, p. 159.

construct state ("in the beginning of"). Even without the preposition *be*, *reshith* in its 50 Old Testament appearances is almost always found in the construct state.

Several scholars express their insights, beginning with J. M. P. Smith.

> Even the student beginning his study of Hebrew is puzzled [by what he sees] here... The easy explanation of the difficulty lies in the fact that [*reshith*] here stands in the construct relation with the following clause. [Smith follows with numerous Old Testament examples, concluding with the synonymous *techillah* in Hosea 1:2]: "At the beginning when Yahweh spoke through Hosea then Yahweh said to Hosea, etc." This case is of especial value for our purposes since the construction...is in principle exactly the same as that of Gen. 1:1-3. [Thus the first verse] is obviously incomplete in and of itself...[10]

Smith's final sentence states the case for the primary scriptural thesis of this study. Speiser agrees:

> Grammatically, this is evidently in the construct state... Thus the sense of this particular initial term is, or should be, "At the beginning of...," or "when," and not "In/At the beginning"; the absolute form with adverbial connotation would be [*bareshith*]. As the text is now vocalized, therefore, the Hebrew Bible starts out with a dependent clause.[11]

The 11th century Jewish scholar Rashi long ago presented that very argument:

> For the passage does not come to teach (us) the order of the (acts of) creation, to say that these (heaven and earth) came first. For if it came to teach us that, it would have been necessary to write: "at first" He created the heavens, etc.; for you have no (occurrence of the word) *reshith* in Scripture, which is not in (the construct state). [Rashi follows with three biblical

---

[10] Smith, *op. cit.*, p. 108. See Appendix for modern translations that hold the construct state.

[11] Speiser, *op. cit.*, p. 12.

> examples] So here also you should propound: as if (it
> were) in the beginning of (God's) creating. [Rashi
> then quotes the same example, Hosea 1:2]...[12]

Another modern commentator, Cohen, says further,

> If the text is rendered literally, the translation is: "in
> the beginning of God's creating the heaven and the
> earth..." This translation is necessary because *reshit'*.
> never means "the beginning" but "the beginning of"
> (cf. Genesis 10:10; Jeremiah 26:1).[13]

Rashi's and Cohen's bold assertions would be disputed by
some Hebrew scholars who insist that *reshith* is found at
least one time (perhaps several) in the absolute state
("the beginning").[14]

Brown, Driver and Briggs in their authoritative lexicon
contradicted their predecessor Gesenius by stating, "[I]n the
beginning when God created [is] to be preferred over the
abs[olute] in the beginning God created."[15]

Thus the quite limited weight of evidence indicates that
the first three words of the Bible, *bereshith bara' Elohim*,
mean (with the Masoretic pointing) literally, "In the
beginning of God created..." The best English expression
to capture the meaning of the opening clause is "When God
began to create..."[16]

---

[12] Rashi, *The Pentateuch and Rashi's Commentary, Genesis, op. cit.*, p. 1.

[13] A. Cohen, *The Soncino Chumash*, Hindhead, Surrey: Soncino Press, 1947, p. 1.

[14] Fields, *op. cit.*, pp. 153-54; Lane, *op. cit.*, pp. 66-67.

[15] Francis Brown, S. R. Driver, Charles A. Briggs, *A Hebrew & English Lexicon of the Old Testament*, Oxford: The Clarendon Press, 1907 (reprinted 1959).

[16] Cf. RSV footnote to Gen. 1:1; C. A. Simpson, "Genesis," *Interpreter's Bible*, Vol. I, Nashville: Abingdon, 1952, p. 466; Cyrus H. Gordon, *Ugaritic Textbook*, Rome: Pontifical Biblical Institute, 1965, p. 56.

The disagreement further concerns the understanding of the verb — that most exciting Hebrew word *bara'*, "to create." Is it participial? Does it mean creation out of nothing? In the Old Testament *bara'* is found 48 times in its simple form, most of these occurrences appearing in Genesis and Isaiah.[17] The word in its simple form is always used with God — never man — as its subject. In addition, "the accusative of material used" (in creating) is never specifically noted. It is truly a majestic word. Thus, at least to the modern mind, the doctrine of *creatio ex nihilo* could possibly be inferred from Gen. 1:1.

This idea however can be defended only with difficulty. As long ago as 1852 William Paul noted, "The most eminent Hebrew scholars are now of opinion that the idea of creation out of nothing cannot be shewn to be inherent in the word *bara'*."[18] Further, "the material used" by God is usually implied by the context, e.g., "I create Jerusalem a rejoicing..." (Isaiah 65:18); "Create in me a clean heart..." (Psalms 51:10); "...that a people yet to be created may praise the Lord" (Psalms 102:18, NASB). In addition, *bara'* is sometimes used synonymously with other Hebrew words for create, form, make, build, produce, order, etc., including Gen. 1:7,16,21, 25,26,27,31 (see also Isaiah 45:7-12,18). There is no basis for assuming that *bara'* denotes a creation out of nothing, even if some commentators insist upon it.

The Masoretic vowel pointings of *bereshith* and *bara'* in

---

[17] James G. Murphy, *A Critical and Exegetical Commentary on the Book of Genesis*, Boston: Estes & Lauriat, 1873, p. 4.

[18] William Paul, *Analysis and Critical Interpretation of the Hebrew Text of the Book of Genesis*, Edinburgh & London: William Blackwood & Sons, 1852, p. 1. Roman Catholic Carroll Stuhlmueller ("The Theology of Creation in Second Isaias," *Catholic Biblical Quarterly*, Vol. 21, 1959) names a few Catholic scholars who "teach *creatio ex nihilo*. However, most authors deny such a teaching..." (p. 462, note).

verse 1 could be emended minimally to indicate definitely a dependent clause. It makes no sense to point either word in such a compromising manner as the Masoretes did many centuries after Genesis was written, so Kittel has proposed a slightly different and quite reasonable pointing which would clearly make the first verse a dependent clause.[19] Without the confusing vocalization there would be no problem; the original Hebrew consonants remain the same. Just one small vowel change in *bereshith* and another in *bara'* would give a clear vocalization, demanding a dependent clause. On the other hand, several slight alternative changes could clearly require a finite quality of *bara'*.

A pertinent sidelight involves Protestant discussions of biblical inerrancy. Beginning with Luther and Calvin and continuing to our day, conservative writers who accept inerrancy tend *not* to include the Masoretic vowel pointings as being without error. The Preface to the RSV notes the translators' usual position:

> The vowel signs... are accepted also in the main, but where a more probable and convincing reading can be obtained by assuming different vowels, this has been done... [T]he vowel points are less ancient and reliable than the consonants.[20]

Thus no final, indisputable resolution is possible unless more information becomes available.

Three synonymous Hebrew words are found in Gen. 1 and 2: *bara'* and *'asah* in chapter 1 and *yatsar* in chapter 2. All three mean to create, to make, to form. All are used together, again synonymously, in Isaiah 45:7-12, 18. *Yatsar* is

---

[19] Rudolph Kittel, *Biblia Hebraica*, Stuttgart, Württembergische: Bibelanstalt, 1937, p. 1, note. But see E. J. Young, *op. cit.*, p. 3; and H. C. Leupold, *Exposition of Genesis*, Grand Rapids: Baker, 1950, p. 41.

[20] *The Revised Standard Version of the Bible*, 2nd ed., Nashville: Thomas Nelson, 1971, p. iv.

the Hebrew word found in Gen. 2:7 when "the LORD God formed man of lumps of ground."[21] Observe that man was *not* created out of nothing, but explicitly "of lumps of ground," yet in chapter 1 the author uses *bara'* of the creation of man — not once but *three times* in verse 27. To suggest man's creation out of nothing in chapter 1 and out of lumps of ground in chapter 2 is absolutely contradictory.

Incidentally, the opening sentence of this *second* creation narrative possesses the same grammatical structure as the proposed initial sentence of Gen. 1: dependent clause ... parenthetic clauses ...main clause. The second opening sentence begins with the dependent clause at 2:4b, "In the day that the LORD God made the earth and the heavens..." Then follows a series of parenthetic clauses. The subject and principal verb of that sentence are not found before verse 7: "...then the LORD God formed [*yatsar*]..." The similarity of sentence structure between the openings of the two creation narratives is impressive. If the two-and-a-half-verse introduction to Gen. 1 seems long and awkward, the opening sentence following Gen. 2:4a is even longer!

The three Hebrew synonyms are translated consistently by modern versions so that the non-Hebrew-reading student can ascertain which verb is being used.[22] *Bara'* is always rendered "create," *'asah* "make" and *yatsar* "form." Speaking through the Old Testament prophets, the Lord often used quite colorful language which can hardly be captured in English translation. Synonymous Hebrew words and phrases appear together in delightfully creative patterns. Isaiah 43:7 displays all three Hebrew words in rapid sequence as God describes his servants, "...whom I created [*bara'*] for my glory, whom I formed [*yatsar*] and made [*'asah*]." Thus to

---

[21] Speiser, *op. cit.*, p. 16.

[22] ASV, RSV, NASB, NEB, NIV, *et al.*

insist that *bara'* demands *creatio ex nihilo* in unwarranted. The varied contexts and synonymous usages of all three Hebrew words indicate otherwise.

Fields, whose exegesis is almost flawless otherwise, begins to use pejorative language when dealing with the proposed dependent clause of Gen. 1:2: "This extreme view... the pantheistic notion...such a translation is very dubious."[23] Actually, Fields never does deal fully with the basic scriptural thesis of this book. His criticisms either are directed toward a pre-Genesis ruin-and-re-creation or impatiently dismiss out-of-hand any view that seems "liberal." His study is weak only at this point, where the evidence weighs against his case.

David Kimchi, the 13th-century Jewish commentator, also does some delicate linguistic footwork to avoid the obvious; but he is so transparent that any student can perceive the fanciful casuistry. Commenting on Isaiah 43:7, Kimchi disagrees with earlier Jewish writers by trying to defend the concept of creation out of nothing.

> I have created him, that is, produced him out of nothing; I have formed him, that is, caused him to exist in a shape or form appointed; I have made him, that is, made the final dispositions and arrangements concerning him.[24]

Medieval and modern piety, whether Jewish or Christian, apparently demands that Gen. 1:1 make God to be *Creator ex nihilo*. One way or another, we seem to insist on retaining the concept.

Gen. 1 adds an additional, almost-synonymous word, *nathan*, meaning "set": "And God *set* them in the firmament of the heavens..." (1:17). This could be translated "made"

---

[23] Fields, *op. cit.*, pp. 161-162.

[24] David Kimchi, quoted in G. H. Pember, *Earth's Earliest Ages*, N.Y.: Fleming H. Revell, 1876, p. 24.

also, as in Gen. 17:5,20 and Exodus 18:25. A fifth synonym, *qanah*, appears in Gen. 4:1 — "I have gotten [created] a man...," from which word Eve named her son Cain. Elsewhere God is always the subject of *qanah* (as He is of *bara'*), and the word is consistently translated "create," "Creator." Still another synonym appears in Gen. 2:22 where the Lord God used the man's rib to "build up" [*banah*] the woman. All six are quite similar in meaning: *nathan, qanah, banah, bara', 'asah, yatsar*. Three additional almost-synonymous words are used in poetic parallelism.[25] There are yet others. Fields lists at least ten different expressions from Gen. 1 and 2 which describe God's creative work.[26]

Verse one includes "...the heavens and the earth..." Normally, when an ancient Hebrew spoke of the heavens, he meant "the sky" and what he saw in it; when he spoke of the earth, he meant "the land" (as opposed to "the sea").[27] Traditionalists cannot accept this fact since it violates their position that God created "the waters" as an implicit part of "the earth."[28] Some commentators feel that the larger context indicates that the author intended to speak of the universe, or at least what we call the Solar System, but there was no such Hebrew word available. They assert that the expression, "the heavens and the earth," is "a description of the organized universe, not of chaos."[29]

---

[25] Bergman, Ringgren, Bernhardt, Botterweck, art. *"bara',"* *Theological Dictionary of the Old Testament*, Vol. II, ed. G. Johannes Botterweck & Helmer Ringgren, trans. John T. Willis, Grand Rapids: Eerdmans, 1975, p. 246.

[26] Fields, *op. cit.*, p. 73.

[27] F. P. Ramsay, *An Interpretation of Genesis*, N.Y.: Neale, 1911, p. 66.

[28] Fields, *op. cit.*, p. 18.

[29] Simpson, *op. cit.*, p. 466.

"[T]he heavens and the earth" is a formula which
always designates the totality of the universe in its
order and beauty. To apply the phrase to a confused
mass is to make it mean its opposite.[30]

Therefore these opening words of chapter 1 appear to
comprise, not an actual creation, but merely an introductory,
temporal clause. The *context* of the entire chapter, however,
is decisive.[31] *If* verse 1 describes an ordered land-sea-sky, the
remainder of the chapter — with its orderly process of
creation so carefully noted — would be redundant. *If* "the
heavens" were completed in verse 1, then the making of "the
firmament" (the sky) in verse 7 seems quite odd, and the
whole creative activity in the heavens on Day Four is utterly
intrusive and repetitious. Likewise, *if* the earth had been
created in verse 1, a strange re-creation is taking place when
once again the earth is formed in verses 9 and 10.

To continue, verse 2 speaks clearly of chaos, an
impossibility if God had just created an orderly world. The
overall context makes the traditional translation absolutely
contradictory. Verse 1 is looking *forward* to the Creation!

---

[30] Blocher, *op. cit.*, p. 64.

[31] Oswald T. Allis in *God Spake by Moses*, (Nutley, N. J.:
Presbyterian & Reformed Publishing Co., 1976, p. 9), says,
incorrectly, "'Create' (*bara*) is a rare word in the Old Testament
[not really: it is found more than 50 times]... It does not
necessarily mean creation *out of nothing*...; but this is clearly
implied." Sadly, Allis is engaging in wishful thinking: it is *not*
"clearly implied"; for implications we look to the context, which
appears to deny *creatio ex nihilo* repeatedly.

E. J. Young and Fields both state (concerning the earlier
discussion of *bereshith*), in defense of the traditional translation,
"In fact, the context favors the absolute state" (Fields, *op. cit.*,
p. 156). Actually, it is the context that almost *destroys* the case
for the LXX/Vulgate/King James interpretation. In reading
these two excellent presentations, the student must be constantly
on guard for the clever insertion of such "axiomatic" statements
that are unproven and undemonstrable.

Further, as that initial verse looks ahead, so Gen. 2:1 looks *backward* to the Creation as described in the previous chapter: "Thus the heavens and the earth were finished, and all the host of them."

Additionally, verse 2 in the Hebrew can hardly stand by itself as a complete sentence. The nouns precede the verbs, which would be abnormal for finite verbs.[32] This suggests strongly a parenthetical quality for verse 2. Actually, the verbs would be superfluous if this were a complete sentence, as the traditional versions render.[33] We find here circumstantial clauses suggesting a translation such as "...the earth having been a desolate chaos..."[34] Thus verse 2 is describing the state of things at the time when God began to create something "good" out of pre-existent chaos.

Finally, the subject and the main verb of the opening sentence of the Bible are found at the beginning of verse 3: "...God said..." Thus we have an introductory temporal clause (verse 1), a parenthetical statement of the existing condition (verse 2), and the initial creative word (verse 3a) — all in one sentence.[35] So involved an opening sentence may seem awkward to us moderns, but it is quite acceptable to the Bible, both Old and New Testaments. Such sentence structure is termed "periodic." As we have already seen, a similar example would be the opening sentence of the second creation narrative in Gen. 2; it is three-and-a-half verses long. Luke opens his Gospel with a four-verse Greek period!

---

[32] Speiser, *op. cit.*, p. 5, note 2; but see Umberto Cassuto, *A Commentary on the Book of Genesis*, trans. Israel Abrahams, Jerusalem: Magnes Press, 1944, p. 19.

[33] Childs, *op. cit.*, p. 32.

[34] Smith, *op. cit.*, p. 110.

[35] Speiser, *op. cit.*, pp. 11-13.

Such an introductory sentence is not at all unusual in the scriptures.[36]

A number of modern Hebrew scholars hold Gen. 1:1 to be a complete sentence, with *bereshith* in the absolute state, largely because of the more than two millennia of tradition (Gunkel, von Rad, Zimmerli, Eichrodt, Cassuto, Westermann).[37] They consider verse 1 to be titular, a headline or summary statement. Verse 2 is then the pre-creation chaos, and verse 3 records God's initial creative effort. And these authors do make a strong case: 2,200 years of versions and transliterations is a formidable objection to overcome. Although this treatise holds otherwise about the syntax of these early verses, still the titular hypothesis is quite compatible with the overall thesis maintained herein. *Creatio ex nihilo* is not a necessary derivative of the traditional translation.

In the light of the foregoing, no student of scripture without a theological ax to grind could consider the Creation to have taken place in verse 1; to conclude otherwise would render all exegesis of scripture absurd. Let us allow scripture to tell us of *creatio ex nihilo* if it will; doctrine must be derived from the written word, not the reverse. Erroneous reasoning as the result of *a priori* assumptions so often leads a student into *ad hoc* scenarios such as the gap or day-age theories.[38]

Biblical exegetes are repeatedly faced with certain problems. The greatest of these problems is the historical

---

[36] For additional complicated syntactical constructions in the Old Testament, see Hasel, *op. cit.*, p. 166.

[37] E. g., von Rad, *op. cit.*, p. 47.

[38] See the chapter, "Concordistic Theories"; also Merrill F. Unger, "Rethinking the Genesis Account of Creation," *Bibliotheca Sacra*, Vol. 115, 1958, p. 28.

gap of centuries between the original writing and the modern reading of the Bible. The cultural and linguistic barriers are immense. The "phenomenon of writing" confronts modern exegetes with a continuing puzzle; that is, the various portions of the Bible were addressed to particular generations, but for centuries have been read by generations not intended (by man) to read them. Thus, as one generation succeeds another, the readers peruse the "text," knowing ever less about the "context."[39] Scripture must be investigated contextually.[40] Credible exegesis of the Old Testament does not permit the intrusion of post-Enlightenment categories of thought!

One of the attributes of God which we learn from other Old Testament scriptures is that *He did not create chaos*. Isaiah 45:18 says of the earth's formation, "He did not create it a formless mass [*tohu*], he formed it to be inhabited!" The succeeding verse adds, "I did not say..., 'Seek me in chaos [*tohu*].'" However, the traditional interpretation of Gen. 1:2 implies that God's initial creation was, crudely, a mess! Examine verse 2: "...and the earth being a *formless waste* and *darkness* being upon the face of the *deep* and the Spirit of God moving over the face of the *waters*..." The five italicized words are all descriptive of chaos. Of all these entities — *tohu, bohu, choshek* (darkness), *tehom* (the deep), and *hamayim* (the waters) — not one is expressly noted in chapter 1 to have been created by God, although numerous other physical entities are specifically named. Waltke reminds us that "No mention is made anywhere in Scripture that God called the unformed, dark, and watery state of

---

[39] Cf. Gene M. Tucker, *Form Criticism of the Old Testament*, Philadelphia: Fortress Press, 1971, chapter 1, "The Form Critical Method."

[40] Hyers, *op. cit.*, p. 2.

verse 2 into existence."[41] Would God have created confusion?
Julius Wellhausen, in attempting to be consistent,
suggested just that![42] C. A. Simpson[43] and G. Ch. Aalders[44]
recently agreed, as have many others through the centuries,
including Gesenius, the great 19th century Hebrew lexicogra-
pher. In their defense, if one accepts the traditional version
of Gen. 1:1, the only logical conclusion in that God created
the chaos of verse 2. John Calvin, that quite logical
Reformer, defended this very interpretation:

> Moses simply intends to assert that the world was not
> perfected at its very commencement, in the manner in
> which it is now seen, but that it was created an empty
> chaos of heaven and earth.[45]

All of these credit God with the chaos of verse 2,
despite the contradictory fact that verse 1 is in language
descriptive of an organized sky-land-sea.[46]   E. J. Young

---

[41] Bruce K. Waltke, "The Creation Account in Genesis 1:1-3,"
Part III, *Bibliotheca Sacra*, July 1975, p. 221. However,
Psalms 104:6 (*if* it refers to the Creation) might indicate that God
had created *tehom*; and Isaiah 45:7 says of the Lord, "I form light
and create [*bara'*] darkness [*choshek*]." Apparently however the
author meant by these statements only that the Lord had
restricted the deep and the darkness to their assigned times
and places. Here *bara'* means "separated," "ordered."

[42] Julius Wellhausen, *Die composition des Hexateuchs* (3rd ed.),
Berlin, 1899, p. 105 (noted in Childs, *op. cit.*, p. 30).

[43] Simpson, *op. cit.*, pp. 467f.

[44] G. Ch. Aalders, *Genesis*, Bible Student's Commentary, Vol. I.
trans. William Heynen, Grand Rapids: Zondervan, 1981, pp. 52f.

[45] John Calvin, *Commentaries on the Book of Genesis*, Vol. I, trans.
John King, Grand Rapids: Eerdmans, 1948, p. 69.

[46] Speiser, *op. cit.*, pp. 12-13; Childs, *op. cit., p. 31; Eichrodt, op.
cit.*, Vol. 2, p. 104, note; Edmond Jacob, *Theology of the Old
Testament*, trans. Arthur W. Heathcote and Philip J. Allcock,
London: Hodder and Stoughton, 1958, p. 144, note.

avoids the difficult issue by insisting that those five Hebrew words of verse 2 do not refer to chaos, but simply "...it was not habitable, not ready for man."[47]   Such exegesis seems casuistic. Consider the negative qualities of *tohu wabohu* in Isaiah 34:11 and Jer. 4:23, and of *tehom* in Psalms 106:9 and Amos 7:4 (cf. Rev. 21:1).

Cyrus H. Gordon says,

> In Genesis 1, the biblical author has sidestepped the embarrassing implication of monotheism, that God is the author of everything, which would make Him the creator of evil as well as good. Instead we read that darkness was in the world before God performed His first creative act: the evoking of light. According to Genesis all of God's creative acts are good; evil is not attributed to Him.[48]

Waltke adds,

> [The *tohu wabohu* of Gen. 1:2] indicates a state of material prior to its creation,...material devoid of order, or without being shaped or formed into something.[49]

All exegetical theories of Gen. 1:1-3 other than the dependent clause are self-contradicting; they contain the seeds of their own invalidation.

The God of the Bible is the very antithesis of chaos. He brings order out of disorder, domesticates the untamed. Consider some analogies. A sculptor chisels a block of shapeless marble to "create" a work of art;[50] a pioneer clears a forest, cultivates and plants it to "create" a farm; an inventor places together discrete components to "create" a

---

[47] E. J. Young, *op. cit.*, pp. 11-14.

[48] Cyrus H. Gordon, "Leviathan: Symbol of Evil", *Biblical Motifs: Origins and Transformations*, ed. Alexander Altmann, Cambridge: Harvard Univ. Press, 1966, p. 1.

[49] Waltke, *op. cit.*, Part III, April 1975, pp. 142-43.

[50] Ramm, *op. cit.*, p. 203.

new and useful product; an interior decorator selects and arranges pieces to "create" a lovely home. Such is the nature of God's creativity. *Creatio ex nihilo* is a concept foreign to the Old Testament!

Although the syntactical issue of Gen. 1:1 remains as controversial as ever — the traditional absolute state (In the beginning...") as opposed to the construct state (In the beginning of...") — because of the weight of evidence, the smaller number of inherent problems, and the overall context of both Gen. 1 and the rest of the Bible, our study will proceed from this point on the assumption that a dependent clause was intended by the biblical author.

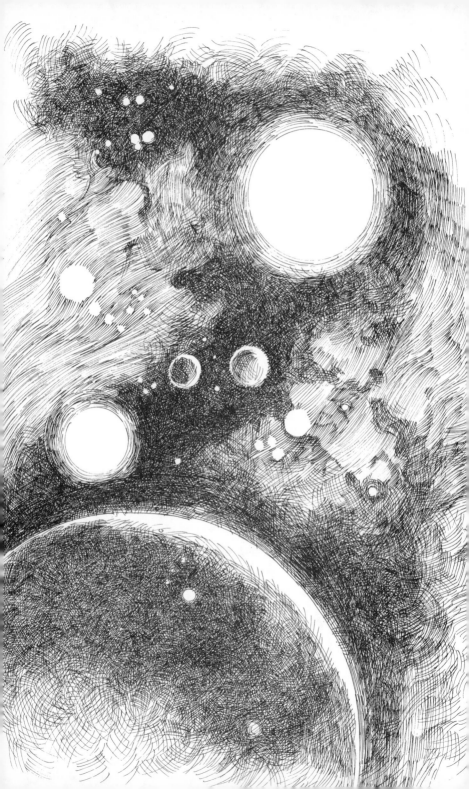

IV ANCIENT HEBRAIC THOUGHT AND THE CONCEPT OF "NOTHING"

We westerners are heirs to Greek culture, with an additional two thousand years-plus of human history and development. We face the problem discussed earlier, the historical and cultural gap. And it is immense.[1] The idea of "nothing" has changed radically. "Nothing" in terms of the zero, the cypher, is a relatively modern concept. The Babylonians of 2000 B.C. (the place and period out of which came Abram the Hebrew), even with their most sophisticated sexagesimal numeral system, still did not grasp the idea of the zero for another two thousand years.[2] Even then, the zero was known only among the limited caste of Babylonian astrologers who used their great mathematical skills to plot and predict from the motions of the visible planets. The first actual recorded use of the zero comes from Ptolemy's *Almagest* about A.D. 140,[3] although in earlier centuries several cultures used a blank space or some distinctive mark to signify a place-value notation (as we also use the zero). But the concept of "nothing" in arithmetic remained undiscovered for centuries, and it resisted popular awareness until the western world had experienced a Renaissance.[4]

---

[1] Ramm, *op. cit.*, pp. 65f, presents a helpful discussion, although he includes a number of unsubstantiated statements.

[2] *Encyclopaedia Britannica*, 15th ed.: Vol. 1, p. 1175; Vol. 11, pp. 639f.

[3] *Ibid.*, Vol. 11, p. 640.

[4] Lancelot Hogben, *Mathematics for the Millions*, N.Y.: W. W. Norton, 1937, Chap. VII, "The Dawn of Nothing, or, How Algebra Began," pp. 283f.

Before the notion of *creatio ex nihilo* could be understood by humans, a philosophical-religious basis had to be
established. This is understood to have occurred in the first
and second Christian centuries as a combination of old and
new ideas began to interact in the Middle East. Zoroastrian
dualism from the east, Greek philosophy from the west, and
Christianity from the center — all conspired together to form
one of the most powerful and persistent heresies during the
two thousand years of Church history: gnosticism. These
new "scientific" teachings excited men's minds, and intelligent, articulate leaders syncretized all they were learning to
propose some complex systems of gnosticism. In the midst of
all this ferment the novel Persian concept of the zero
appeared. And, as far as can be ascertained by this research,
the famous gnostic Basilides first proposed *creatio ex nihilo*.[5]

We learn about Basilides primarily from Hippolytus, the
3rd century Bishop of Rome who was later martyred for his
faith. An Alexandrian of the early 2nd century, Basilides had
been nurtured in Iranian Zoroastrianism, having been heavily
exposed also to Greek philosophical and Egyptian Christian
influences.[6] These three cultures provided the perfect "mix"
for a doctrine of *creatio ex nihilo*. "Basilides," says Haardt,
"in order to give the appearance of having discovered
something deeper and truer, extended his doctrine beyond

---

[5] Edwin Tenney Brewster, *Creation*, Indianapolis: Bobbs-Merrill,
1927, p. 53: "But did [the author of Gen. 1] mean by *bara* to create
out of nothing? Unquestionably, by about the beginning of the
Christian Era, thanks apparently to the great Gnostic Bacilides,
bara had taken on that meaning. But in 500 B.C. *bara* meant
'to separate,' 'to cut out,' 'to manufacture.'"

[6] Gilles Quispel, *Gnostic Studies*, I, Istanbul: Nederlands Instituut
voor het Nabije Oosten, 1974, pp. 103f.

limits."[7] Hippolytus writes concerning this novel doctrine of
creatio ex nihilo,

> (Time) was, says (Basilides), when there was *nothing.*
> Not even, however, did that nothing constitute
> anything of existent things;...without any quibbling,
> it is altogether nothing... I affirm then, he says, that it
> was "altogether nothing."[8]

Now, for the first time, the Graeco-Roman scholarly world
could conceive of creation out of nothing. Many educated
Christians would have accepted *creatio ex nihilo* immediately
because it seemed to exalt the true God. It is important
however to remember its heretical source. Important also is it
to perceive in this quotation from Hippolytus that, although
the bishop flourished as late as the 3rd century, creation out
of nothing was obviously still foreign to his thinking.

As we have seen then, prior to the early 2nd century even
the educated ancients (apart from a select group of Indian
and Persian astrologers) could not imagine what we moderns
call "nothing." In order to understand the Old Testament
world view, we must practice Hebraic thinking: we must
conceive of a creation without a zero. The Hebraic nothing
was, rather, *chaos* — *tohu wabohu, tehom,* a jungle perhaps,
or a desert — simply a place that is uninhabitable, unusable
by man. And God in his creativity made a portion of this
water-covered planet habitable. He "ordered" it. When in
Gen. 1:4 '...God separated the light from the darkness" He
was establishing order between the "good" light and the "evil"
darkness. As Jesus stated with great awareness to those

---

[7] Robert Haardt, *Gnosis: Character and Testimony*, trans. J. F.
Hendry, Leiden: E. J. Brill, 1971, p. 41.

[8] Hippolytus, "The Refutation of All Heresies," VII, viii, *Ante-
Nicene Fathers*, Vol. V, ed. Alexander Roberts & James
Donaldson, Buffalo: Christian Literature Publishing Co., 1885,
p. 103.

arresting Him in Gethsemane, "But this is your hour, and the power of darkness" (Luke 22:53b).

Of all the many dozens of ancient creation myths worldwide (and it may be that there is a solid kernel of truth, albeit distorted, in every one of them), not one depicts *creatio ex nihilo*.[9] Every ancient pagan cosmogony describes a process of formation by which a god (or, gods) created the earth out of pre-existent material — not a passive material, but usually a body of substance possessing an evil, rebellious personality.

The Bible of course differs sharply from other ancient cosmogonies in that it reveals events in Earth's natural history as "...men moved by the Holy Spirit spoke from God" (2 Peter 1:21). 2 Peter also asserts, "We did not follow cleverly devised myths" (1:16a). We today must ascertain that biblical truth in its ancient context, to learn what the authors, inspired by God, were trying to tell their contemporaries, *not* their descendants.

20th century Christians have little idea how extensively modern rationalistic and uniformitarian thought has affected their world view. Many of us assert boldly that we believe the "whole" Bible to be true, all the while viewing it through rationalistic "glasses." We unconsciously try to demythologize the scriptures, questioning the reality of Satan and demonic spirits, miracles, healings, and nearly every other biblical and contemporary manifestation of supernaturalism, scarcely

---

[9] Dwardu Cardona, "Creation and Destruction," *Kronos*, Vol. IV, No. 3, p. 73, "Forum": "In no myth has ancient man ever deluded himself into thinking that the Earth was created of nothing." Lucretius, the 1st century B.C. Roman poet and philosopher, stated, "We shall begin with this first principle, nothing is ever gotten out of nothing by divine power." "On the Nature of Things," Book I, 146, trans. H. A. J. Munro, *Great Books of the Western World*, Vol. 12, Chicago: Encyclopaedia Britannica, 1952, pp. 2, 3.

realizing that the Bible had already been demythologized when it was written.

As many scholars have pointed out to us deceived westerners, most of the Old Testament was written *in* Hebrew, *by* Hebrews, *to* Hebrews, *within* a Hebrew culture. The Septuagint, which was for centuries the Old Testament for Christians, is Greek, western, the product of a blending of the two cultures. The LXX is quite different in many respects from the text inherited from the Masoretes. Rashi's is a call back to the original intent of the opening verses of the Hebrew Genesis, resulting as well (as we shall see) in a much more plausible exposition scientifically.

This presentation is also a call to creationists to believe *everything* the Bible says about creation. Post-Enlightenment reinterpretation of scripture usually leads to error. We must permit the Bible to speak to us!

Not included in the scope of this book is the forming of the animal kingdom, those creatures to whom God gave *nephesh*, life itself. But let us digress momentarily. Scientific creationists today often state that everything God made in Genesis was accomplished by processes that are no longer operative in the earth. It is true of course that the Spirit of God completed his initial creative work in those six days. But Isaiah 48:7 says, "They ["new things"] are created [*bara'*] now, not long ago..." As may be observed in this verse, a similar creation terminology is used in Isaiah to predict the future re-establishment of the Jewish state.

And the same creative (*bara'*) power is available as needed today; for even as Jesus used his power twenty centuries ago, we see Him still today creating eyeballs where there were none, new ear drums, a new hand, even hair on a bald head. The physically dead once again are often given God's unique gift of *nephesh*. Only our rationalistic "blinders" prevent us from perceiving that the same personal

Spirit and the same natural forces and processes involved in the Genesis Creation *are operative today*. We moderns are not so far removed from Creation Week after all!

V THE NEW TESTAMENT AND CREATIO EX NIHILO

Although it seems to be nearly impossible to defend *creatio ex nihilo* in the Old Testament, the New Testament does appear to speak forthrightly about a doctrine of creation out of nothing.

But does it? Certainly every student of the Bible has been awaiting a discussion of Romans 4:17 and Hebrews 11:3.

First, Paul tells in Romans 4:17 of a "...God ...who ...calls into existence the things that do not exist." Then the Letter to the Hebrews 11:3 says, "The world was created by the word of God, so that what is seen was made out of things which do not appear." What of these apparent biblical affirmations of *creatio ex nihilo*? Is this perhaps an example of "progressive revelation"?

Once again, we must beware of perceiving scripture (written in the thought forms of a generation immersed in Platonic philosophy) through our 20th century uniformitarian eyes. The author of Hebrews did not intend what we understand today by "things which do not appear." In recent centuries we have come to understand it to mean nothing — zero! But note carefully: Hebrews 11:3 speaks of "things," not nothings. By that statement our *Old Testament* ancestors would have meant unformed things, confused things, empty habitations, wild, desolate, chaotic — yes, even the Hebrew words of Gen. 1:2 — *tohu wabohu, tehom.* But by the time of the *New Testament* the author of Hebrews spoke of invisible (or, heavenly) things, but things nevertheless (Col. 1:16). A most important point for comprehending the New Testament concept of creation: Greek Platonism had long since provided for Jews and Christians the philosophical basis for distinguishing things visible (earthly) from things invisible (heavenly).   Hebrews 11:3 is not speaking of *ex nihilo* creation, but rather a creation of physical things *out of* spiritual things.

Even as early as the 3rd century B.C. the LXX translators, already influenced by Alexandrian Platonism, translated the *tohu wabohu* of Gen. 1:2, not as "formless chaos" or anything similar, but rather as "invisible and unordered." The Greek word "chaos" was available to them, but they understood *tohu wabohu* more nearly in Platonic terms.   Paul demonstrates such thinking by the manner in which he spoke of the Creation in Col. 1:16: "...[F]or in [Christ] all things were created, in heaven and on earth, visible and invisible..."   These final words are Platonic.

Second, Paul's reference in Romans 4:17 to God's calling "into existence the things that do not exist" can be explained by an analogous quotation from the great Apostle.   He says in 1 Cor. 1:28, "God chose what is low and despised in the world, even things that are not, to bring to nothing things that are..."   To try to understand this verse in 20th century western terms is extremely awkward.   "...[T]hings that are not, to bring to nothing things that are..."!   Paul's assertion could even strike the modern mind as incomprehensible. Only by studying the statement in its context do we perceive that Paul, who thought in both Greek and Jewish terms, means that "people or institutions currently held in great esteem will be brought down to being disgraced or confused or destroyed," certainly not to what we consider "nothing" today.   We might even say, with the author of Gen.1, "brought down from order to disorder."[1]

---

[1] Cf. Isaiah 34:12; 40:23; 1 Cor. 6:13, 15:24,26; 2 Thes. 2:8.   Cf. Gerhard Delling, art. in *Theological Dictionary of the New Testament*, Vol. I, ed. Gerhard Kittel, trans. Geoffrey W. Bromiley, Grand Rapids: Eerdmans, 1964, pp. 452-54.

Paul's expression in Romans 4:17 could also be explained analogously by a clever mechanic who takes junk parts and builds an acceptable automobile. Modern Americans might say, "He created something out of nothing." No one using this colloquialism could possibly be thinking of *creatio ex nihilo*. Likewise, God takes "nobodies" and makes them "somebodies." And those who think they are "somebodies" God brings down to becoming "nobodies" (as in 1 Cor. 1:28).

Thus we could state that, on the basis of the foregoing, regardless of how Gen. 1:1 is translated, the sense is still the same, whether derived from the Hebraic rendition or the Septuagint/Vulgate/King James tradition. The correct interpretation depends not merely upon the translation, but even more on understanding the ancients' concept of nothing.

There is a third relevant — and most important — New Testament reference to Creation. 2 Peter 3:5 is quite explicit about the meaning of the early verses of Genesis. "By the word of God heavens existed long ago, and an earth formed out of water and by means of water..." The author's choice of "formed" is the perfect participle (as found in Col. 1:17b), dependent upon the finite verb "existed." It means that the earth had already been "framed and possessing existence." The writer *knows* there was pre-existent matter. This verse is a most perceptive New Testament commentary on Gen. 1:2; it must be dealt with by those who would demand a New Testament doctrine of creation out of nothing.

Other New Testament scriptures, such as John 1:1; Eph. 3:9; and Col. 1:15-17, may be thought to allude to *ex nihilo*, but every one merely refers (as far as creation is concerned) back to Gen. 1 and 2, the creation out of something.

Such is the New Testament witness to the Creation. To repeat, the Bible knows nothing of *creatio ex nihilo*.

WISDOM OF SOLOMON

PHILO

GAMALIEL

II ENOCH

THE SHEPHERD OF HERMAS

Constitutions of the Holy Apostles

IRENAEUS

TERTULLIAN

ORIGEN

AUGUSTINE

THE MACARIES

VI THE ANCIENT COMMENTATORS

The Greek Septuagint, we might say, is a commentary on Gen. 1:1-3 merely by the way it was translated. We also find some ancient Jewish and Christian references to the Creation apart from the canonical scriptures and the versions. The evidence conforms rather closely to what we have found in the three primary New Testament references.

The late 2nd century B. C. apocryphal 2 Maccabees contains a mother's admonition to her son: "Look at the heaven and the earth and see everything that is in them, and recognize that God did not make them out of things that existed" (7:28). Some modern commentators feel this verse is the first ancient reference to *creatio ex nihilo*. Such an interpretation is highly questionable however, for it serves only to remind us of Paul's later statement in Romans 4:17, which was discussed in the previous chapter. Neither this 2nd century B.C. Jewish mother nor the scribe who immortalized her courageous speech could have comprehended what we understand today by the concept of nothing. The implication of her statement is that God made "the heaven and the earth" of spiritual "things" — an obvious example of Platonic thinking.

On the other hand, the apocryphal Wisdom of Solomon, dating from within a generation of 2 Maccabees, tells clearly of "...your all-powerful hand which created the world out of formless matter" (11:17a). The Wisdom of Solomon again confirms the ancient Hebraic intention that the Creation took place out of pre-existent material.

Philo of Alexandria, an Alexandrian Jewish con-

temporary of Jesus of Nazareth, was so thoroughly hellenized
that he conceived, with the Greeks, of the great antiquity
(perhaps, eternity) of matter.[1] *Creatio ex nihilo* was foreign to
Philo.

Following the A.D. 70 destruction of Jerusalem, Rabbi
Gamaliel II stated that God in Gen. 1 created the earth out of
pre-existent material which, although not expressly mentioned in scripture, He had created in the first place.[2] The
rabbi was close to the truth.

At some unknown time in the early centuries of this era
there appeared an anonymous Jewish writing known as 2
Enoch, or The Book of the Secrets of Enoch. The mysterious
author, putting words in the mouth of God, says,

> Before anything existed at all, from the very begin-
> ning, whatever is I created from non-being into being,
> and from invisible things into the visible... Before any
> visible things had come into existence...I...moved
> around in the invisible things... Yet I did not find
> rest, because everything was not yet created. And I
> thought up the idea of establishing a foundation, to
> create a visible creation. And I commanded..., "Let
> one of the invisible things come out visibly!" (24:2 -
> 25:1).[3]

Here are seen clear examples of Platonic thinking — the visible
created out of the invisible, precisely as we find it in Romans
4:17; Hebrews 11:3; and 2 Maccabees 7:28.

A few pertinent references appear in the early Church
Fathers. The Shepherd of Hermas dates from the first half of

---

[1] James Hastings, *The Great Texts of the Bible*, Vol. I, N.Y.:
Charles Scribner's Sons, 1911, p. 28.

[2] Georges Vadja, "Notice sommaire sur l'interpretation de
Genèse 1:1-3 dans le judaisme post-biblique," *In Principio:
Interpretation des Premier Versets de la Genèse*, Paris: Etudes
Augustiennes, 1973, pp. 29f. (Noted in Blocher, *op. cit.*, p. 65).

[3] James H. Charlesworth, ed., *The Old Testament Pseudepigrapha,*
Vol. I, Garden City, N.Y.: Doubleday, 1983, pp. 25-27.

the 2nd century. The unknown author describes the "God who dwells in heaven and created the things that are from that which is not..."[4] Again, the Shepherd is thinking in terms similar to Romans and Hebrews and the creation of "visible" things out of "invisible" things, whose original quality was "that which is not," heavenly rather than earthly.

The ancients of this period — in keeping with reigning Platonic philosophy — seemed to distinguish, not as we do today, between "something" and "nothing," but rather, between *types* of "things" — things visible and things invisible.[5] For Jews and Christians the basic contrast would be "things earthly" from "things heavenly." Four centuries of hellenistic exposure affected Jewish thinking deeply — perhaps not so much in actual religious practices, but most certainly metaphysically and philosophically. Jewish (and later, Christian), writings of the period (300 B.C. to A.D. 200) are strongly colored by the Platonic world view.

The Constitutions of the Holy Apostles, from the 2nd or 3rd century, says that God "...in the beginning did reduce into order the disordered parts."[6] This valuable teaching depicts tersely that six-day primeval struggle, again describing a creation out of existing material.

Irenaeus (late 2nd century) provides the first explicit reference to *creatio ex nihilo* in Christian literature. But Irenaeus is thoroughly Greek, and he follows the apparent "father" of *ex nihilo*, the gnostic Basilides, by some years. In

---

[4] "The Shepherd of Hermas", I, 1,6, *The Apostolic Fathers*, Vol. 6, trans. Graydon Snyder, Camden: Thomas Nelson, 1968, p. 28.

[5] Cf. Thorlief Boman's discussion of "non-being" in both Greek and Old Testament Hebrew thought, *Hebrew Thought Compared with Greek*, Philadelphia: Westminster Press, 1960, pp. 55-58.

[6] "Constitutions of the Holy Apostles," Book VII, 34: *Ante-Nicene Fathers, op. cit.*, Vol. VII, p. 472.

"Against Heresies" Irenaeus is lashing out at one of the numerous gnostic systems:

> While men indeed, cannot make anything out of nothing, but only out of matter already existing, yet God is in this point preeminently superior to men, that He Himself called into being the substance of His creation, when previously it had no existence.[7]

Now the scene of the debate moves *inside* the Church. Although the God of the Bible may have been perceived as being more exalted and almighty by the appropriation of *ex nihilo*, not all the Fathers would accept it. Some of them were aware of its suspect origin and, in addition, the new concept of "nothing" required a radical philosophical adjustment in their thinking.

Tertullian however, following Irenaeus by only one generation, considered creation out of nothing to be orthodoxy. The argument over *ex nihilo* raged between two obviously-brilliant Christian teachers of Carthage — Tertullian and Hermogenes.[8] We read only one side of the debate — Tertullian's — so we probably have received a distorted presentation of his opponent's propositions. Tertullian begins with an *ad hominem* attack upon Hermogenes, which should immediately raise the reader's suspicions about the quality of the author's argument. The crusty Tertullian then launches into his typical vitriolic attack with a quite involved and not always consistent logic.

> ...In every operation...there must be three names mentioned...— the person of the maker, the sort of thing which is made, and the material of which it is formed. If the material is not mentioned, while the work and the maker of the work are both mentioned,

---

[7] Irenaeus, "Against Heresies," Book II, x,4: *ibid.*, Vol. I, p. 370.

[8] Tertullian, "Against Hermogenes": *ibid.*, Vol. III, pp. 477-502. The subtitle of his treatise is "Containing an argument against his opinion that matter is eternal."

it is manifest that He made the world out of nothing.[9] A most illogical argument to be sure! Further, Tertullian's exegesis is poor, for we have already seen that the material out of which God made the Earth is indeed noted in Gen. 1:2 and 2 Peter 3:5. Hermogenes must surely have reminded his opponent of that fact. Paradoxically, Tertullian proceeds to contradict himself in his next chapter, admitting that

...scripture has *not* expressly declared that all things were made out of nothing...[10] [italics added]

And there it is. This entire historical presentation could rest on that one mere statement. Tertullian's admission is most important to our modern understanding of how *ex nihilo* began to infiltrate the Christian Church. At least Tertullian is honest enough to face what modern exegetes rarely do — that creation out of nothing is not mentioned anywhere in scripture. Probably the zero-concept was so novel that Tertullian was as yet unable to think of it as merely an implicit part of his world view. Today the idea of nothing is merely assumed in western culture.

So the new concept of *creatio ex nihilo* took many of the Church Fathers by storm. Augustine however was hesitant to accept it. He knew the pagan sources of *ex nihilo*, having for years been a keen student of philosophy. His writings indicate his own struggle, and Augustine's final position was similar to one that will be proposed later: "Although the world has been made of some material, that very same material must have been made out of nothing."[11] Augustine was thinking of "material" which had a pre-biblical origin — *ex nihilo*! And he was probably correct.

---

[9] *Ibid.*, Chapter XX, p. 489.

[10] *Ibid.*, Chapter XXI, p. 489.

[11] Augustine, "De Genesi contra Manichaeos," Book 1, vi; (noted in White, *op. cit.*, pp. 5,26).

The early 3rd century Church Father, Origen, "...held that God's creative activity is without beginning or end, and that an infinity of worlds has preceded this."[12] Like the quite hellenized Philo before him, Origen held to a number of pagan Greek concepts, and he is atypical among ante-Nicene Christian writers. But even the Jewish rabbis of the same period sometimes held similar views. The *Genesis Rabba*, a 5th century Jewish Palestinian writing, also speaks of earlier worlds created and destroyed by God. In fact, some of the Jewish Midrashic commentaries on the Creation are so fanciful that they hardly deserve to be termed mythological.[13] The idea of other, prior worlds is a common human heritage. When a pagan mythology tells of a destruction of previous worlds however, it includes the Flood as one of those destructions and the subsequent world order as a re-creation. A modern Bible student would not conceive of the Flood in those terms. Creation to our minds is quite different from any of the ancient views, biblical or non-biblical.

Caedmon, the uneducated herdsman of 7th century Britain, shared his vision of Genesis and related narratives, all set to music. The Venerable Bede recorded Caedmon's Anglo-Saxon verse. The simple herdsman's understanding of creation was similar to that of other ancients. According to the singing Caedmon, God had long since created the earth, but it was not yet created ready for habitation. The six days of Gen. 1 describes the second creation of the earth as we know it. Caedmon therefore in his heavenly vision pictured a pre-existent earth, created earlier by God but as yet unfit for habitation by man, a picture quite similar to that of

---

[12] Brewster, *op. cit.*, p. 96. Origen's view is expounded in his "De Principiis," *Ante-Nicene Fathers*, Vol. IV, *op. cit.*

[13] Robert Graves & Raphael Patai, *Hebrew Myths, the Book of Genesis*, Garden City, N.Y.: Doubleday, 1964, pp. 34f.

Augustine.[14]

Throughout the Middle Ages Christian writers expressed divergent beliefs. Some believed in *creatio ex nihilo*; others chose a creation out of existing matter.[15] The rediscovery of Aristotle by the medieval Scholastics brought a resurgence of the concept of prior worlds into the Church. Some Christian writers even adopted the idea of the eternity of matter as they tried to "baptize" Aristotle into the faith; but Thomas Aquinas, foremost of the Scholastics, wouldn't accept it. Departing from Aristotle at this point, Aquinas opted strongly for *ex nihilo*.[16]

The Reformers too were uniformly committed to *creatio ex nihilo*, and so the doctrine arrived in the modern Church fully clothed — hallowed, unalterable.

Remaining for centuries in the quiet backwater of biblical scholarship was the 11th century Rashi's call to return to the ancient Hebraic understanding of Gen. 1:1-3. Even contemporary liberal commentators are quite divided on Rashi's exegesis. And the vast majority of Bible students still honestly feel that any interpretation other than creation from nothing would demean the Almighty God. John Pearson, the well-read 17th century English bishop, states the case for all who protest against the idea of the pre-existence of matter.

> For if some real and material being must be presupposed by indispensable necessity, without which God could not cause any thing to be, then is not he independent in his actions, nor of infinite power and absolute activity, which is contrary to the divine

---

[14] Fields, *op. cit.*, pp. 29-30.

[15] Brewster, *op. cit.*, p. 96.

[16] Haber, *op. cit.*, p. 26.

perfection... So doth it contradict his all sufficiency.[17] It is noted forcefully however that the bishop appeals, not to scripture, but to human logic and religious piety. This treatise is an appeal to scripture.

---

[17] John Pearson, *An Exposition of the Creed*, rev. W. S. Dobson, N.Y.: D. Appleton, 1844, p. 81.

VII SCIENTISM

Some readers nurtured in evolutionary thought might describe this book as "anti-science." Such a pejorative epithet is inappropriate; I am, rather, "anti-scientistic."

Scientism is the attempt to extend currently popular scientific theories into other cultural disciplines. Scientism's zealots in every generation imagine that somehow "man" is being replaced by "modern man"; improved education and up-to-date scientific knowledge are releasing us from superstitious bondage. Such efforts to "reform" other disciplines through "modern science" are apparently quite ancient.

The discipline with which we are now concerned is theology. Scientism invades the Church in any generation in which currently-held scientific theories appear to conflict with theology. Christian leaders who are embarrassed by certain "unscientific" aspects of biblical Christianity's unique, scandalous faith will then attempt to syncretize the two disciplines with unbridled enthusiasm. Such pioneering efforts toward concord by prominent philosophers and theologians has, throughout Church history, seemed to fascinate Christian intellectuals, but the end result is always an attenuation of revealed truth.

Gnosticism formed the first such scientistic attempt within Christendom. Already incipient in the Graeco-Roman world before the Church's birth at Pentecost, gnosticism clearly portrayed itself as superior science. "The very nature of Gnosticism...suggests a very strong prevailing spirit of

scientism."[1] Gnostics were an intellectual elite; they claimed
to have been "enlightened" — and thus they destroyed for
early Church use a perfectly good Christian word.[2] Even
those Christian leaders who rejected this powerful heresy
were deeply affected by it philosophically; gnosticism clearly
captured the pagan spirit of the 2nd and 3rd centuries. There
was a good basis for Irenaeus' statement that Simon of
Samaria founded gnosticism:[3] like Simon, its teachers
attempted to combine three claims — esoteric knowledge, a
"scientific" understanding of reality, and the power of the
Christians' Holy Spirit.

Bringing with him the mathematics of the Magi and their
zero-concept, the gnostic Basilides must have been an
impressive teacher. *Creatio ex nihilo* was novel, and, as the
idea percolated within the world view of Platonism and, very
shortly, Neoplatonism, it seemed so scientific! Basilides
unwittingly gave the Church a doctrine that, to the human
mind, might make her Creator appear yet more unique and
all-powerful. Although *ex nihilo's* near-total adoption
required some centuries, the final result was inevitable.

During its two millennia Church history displays three
prominent scientistic errors that arose under the guise of
"modern science." All have been so powerful as to be nearly
impossible to dislodge. In the 2nd century, as we have seen, it
was gnosticism, with its superior "science," bringing among
its many errors the teaching of *creatio ex nihilo*. In recent

---

[1] G. Van Groningen, *First Century Gnosticism*, Leiden: E. J. Brill,
1967, p. 18. Although Van Groningen's work has some serious
weaknesses, yet he carefully documents gnosticism's "scientistic"
basis.

[2] John 1:9; Eph. 1:18; 3:9; Heb. 6:4; 10:32.

[3] Acts 8:9-24. Irenaeus, "Against Heresies," Book I, 27:4;
Early Christian Fathers, Philadelphia: Westminster Press,
1953, p. 368.

years the prominent liberal theologian Paul Tillich had been called a "gnostic."[4] Modern liberalism in the Church is highly scientistic and quite gnostic: many liberal scholars have attempted to discover a "Jesus of history" as distinct from a "Christ of faith"; and they continue to search for an imaginary "God's word" within "the word." Liberalism further synthesizes the Bible and contemporary scientific theory to formulate an implausible "theistic evolution," a syncretistic philosophy alien to both Bible and science.

During the medieval centuries Aristotelianism, with its concept of concrete reality, supplemented the traditional Neoplatonism amid a similar breathtaking excitement in the Roman Catholic scholarly world — again, as the result of scientism. Aristotelianism had filtered through Byzantine scholars to the Arabs, and thence to the western Church's Scholastics. Within a brief time this ancient pagan philosophy utterly dominated the science of the western Church. Galileo's 17th century affliction was actually Aristotelian science in the Italian universities. The Roman Church has yet to remove Aristotelianism from its Thomistic theology. Calvinism too has its philosophical roots in Aristotle; in his massive biblical commentary John Calvin skipped hurriedly (six brief paragraphs in 22 sizable volumes) through the supernatural "gifts of the Spirit" in 1 Corinthians 12 and deliberately omitted the highly supernatural Book of Revelation.[5]

Third, the 19th century dawned upon a Protestant Church in turmoil, fighting a losing battle over the issue of antisupernaturalism. Antisupernaturalism gave birth to two rebellious children in the Church. One of the two offspring,

---

[4] Van Groningen, *op. cit.*, p. 186.

[5] John Calvin, *Commentary on the Epistles of Paul the Apostle to the Corinthians*, trans. John Pringle, Grand Rapids: Baker, reprinted 1979.

modern liberalism, influenced by the rationalism of the Enlightenment, promptly denied the biblical record of miracles.

In the other cradle, educated evangelicals increasingly suffered great anguish, attempting to retain their faith while accepting what "modern science" was telling them. Tragically, a few Christian leaders began acceding to this new scientism which denied the existence of miracles — not quite becoming totally rationalistic, but inconsistently affirming the *biblical* miracles while denying *contemporary* miracles! It is called dispensationalism;[6] during the 19th century this type of antisupernaturalism spread quickly among theologians of Reformed persuasion (because of Calvin's philosophical roots in Aristotelianism).

Today dispensationalism is stronger than ever in the Church; the average Christian layman has been victimized by this strange inconsistency too. Dispensationalist thinking now permeates denominations that have never even heard such a word. Thus 20th century creationists of antisupernaturalistic persuasion are logically required to insist — with no scriptural basis — that God's creative work of Gen. 1 was accomplished under physical laws that no longer operate. Scientistic antisupernaturalism afflicts not only creation science, but the broader Church of Jesus Christ wherever it has been affected by western culture.

Why hadn't the distinctive tenets of modern dispensationalism been taught centuries earlier? Simply, because the western world had not yet experienced the Enlightenment. Enlightenment thinking (or, the *reaction to* Enlightenment thinking) forms the basis for the novel aspects of dispensationalism.

---

[6] Not to be confused with the strictly limited *biblical* concept of two dispensations, so vital to Reformed theology, e.g., 2 Cor. 3:7-11; Eph. 1:9,10; Heb. 9,10.

We should note carefully that all three philosophies — gnosticism, Aristotelianism, dispensationalism — were *unbiblical* intrusions into the Church by the world, each one arising right on schedule, following the secular triumph of "modern science." Scientistic heresies are almost impossible to dislodge; all three mentioned above remain firmly entrenched, and their adherents tend to become quite emotional when opposed. We do well to remember the words of Westermann, quoted earlier: "We have some extremely deeply rooted notions regarding the creation of the world and of man which...do not come from the text of the Bible, but from the history of its interpretation."[7] Scientism, with its erroneous apriorism, continues to cripple man's quest for truth.

---

[7] Westermann, *op. cit.*, p. 1.

VIII CONCORDISTIC THEORIES

As we have just observed, countless writers have tried for centuries to reconcile the Bible with what they have perceived in the natural world around them. Augustine wrestled with it; the medieval Scholastics dealt with it by determinedly conflating contradictory philosophies; devout Christians of scientific bent during the past three centuries especially have agonized over the seeming contradictions. Christians who think of the biblical creation narratives as being in conflict with the "real" natural history of the world have often attempted to re-interpret scripture to bring "theology" in line with "geology." Each one who has succumbed to the *scientistic* temptation to force a portion of Gen. 1 to mean anything other than its clear intent does so in order to achieve "concord" — a harmony with conclusions derived from the *perceived* natural data. He has developed a concordistic theory.

I have to confess to such attempts in my early years as a Christian. I felt quite justified in doing so. After all, I was defending God! Nor had I yet discovered that the whole Bible is really true: it actually is God's word!

One concordistic approach to creation is the restitution hypothesis, popularly known as the gap theory. Attributed to Martin Luther[1] as well as the early 17th century Episcopius[2] (but without specific references cited for either), the theory later seemed to be required in order to explain the fossils that

---

[1] Brewster, *op. cit.*, p. 152.

[2] Delitzsch, *op. cit.*, p. 79.

were being uncovered in growing numbers. The first clear citation of the gap theory appeared about 1776.[3] But it was not popularized until the 19th century.

In 1814 a Scottish minister named Thomas Chalmers became caught up in the intellectual ferment concerning prehistoric time scales. He also wished to believe what his King James Bible told him. Although Chalmers was a superb scholar-scientist-minister, he too was apparently unaware of the medieval Jewish commentaries that shed the light he needed on Genesis. Nor did he dig deeply into the original Hebrew as, of course, the great linguistic tools we possess today were unavailable to him. The great Glasgow clergyman also chose to accept uncritically what the gentlemen-scientists of the early 19th century were saying about an "old" earth. Emerging uniformitarianism was creating quite a stir among Christian students. Chalmers tried to marry his strong biblicism to a desire to be a "modern" pastor and scholar.

So he suggested a compromise — an *ad hoc* proposal — which placed a "gap" of millions (or later, billions) of years between Gen. 1:1 and 1:2. The King James Version reads, "In the beginning God created the heaven and the earth." Chalmers proposed that this "event" was succeeded by a time gap of many millennia. Then, a few thousand years ago, God took up the tools of creation once again, and verse 3 and the rest of the Bible follow consecutively.

> My own opinion, as published in 1814, is that it (Gen. 1:1) forms no part of the first day — but refers to a period of indefinite antiquity when God created the worlds out of nothing. The commencement of the first day's work I hold to be the moving of God's Spirit upon the face of the waters. We can allow geology the amplest time...without infringing even on

---

[3] Ramm, *op. cit.*, p. 196, note. Ramm details the development of the gap theory, pp. 196f.

the literalities of the Mosaic record..."[4]
This compromise was embraced by the sectarian J. N. Darby, one of the early elders of the Plymouth Brethren, and was popularized during the latter half of the 19th century by G. H. Pember and by the early 20th century Scofield Reference Bible.

> It is thus clear that the second verse of Genesis describes the earth as a ruin; but there is no hint of the time which elapsed between creation and this ruin. Age after age may have rolled away, and it was probably during their course that the strata of the earth's crust were gradually developed. Hence we see that geological attacks upon the Scriptures are altogether wide of the mark, are a mere beating of the air. There is room for any length of time between the first and second verses of the Bible. And again; since we have no inspired account of the geological formations, we are at liberty to believe that they were developed just in the order in which we find them. The whole process took place in preadamite times, in connection, perhaps, with another race of beings, and, consequently, it does not at present concern us.[5]

While the world of biblical and scientific creationist scholarship largely ignores Chalmers' gap theory, his proposal has enjoyed an ever-growing popularity among some fundamentalist Christians.[6]

> The inclusion of this theory in the Scofield Bible is most unfortunate, for it has led so many into believing a theory which was tailored to harmonize science in its

---

[4] William Hanna, *Posthumous Works of Thomas Chalmers*, Vol. I, N.Y.: Harper, 1849, p. 1.

[5] Pember, *op. cit.*, p. 28.

[6] See, e.g., R. O. Corvin, *Home Bible Study Course*, Vol. 1, Charlotte: PTL Club, 1976, p. 1.; Vol. 5, p. 1; also LeBaron W. Kinney, *Acres of Rubies*, N.Y.: Loizeaux Brothers, 1942, pp. 157-9.

present fluid form and the Bible in its immutable form.[7]

Most biblical commentators will not even mention the restitution hypothesis or, if they do, it receives scant but scornful notice. An example is Skinner: "The view that verse 1 describes an earlier creation of heaven and earth, which were reduced to chaos and then refashioned, needs no refutation."[8] Skinner is implying that the gap theory has no basis in scripture.

Again, the restitution hypothesis is an *ad hoc* explanation. Such explanations necessarily appear whenever one or more of our basic assumptions is/are incorrect. The problem is two-sided. The first erroneous assumption leading to the gap theory is biblical traditionalism instead of careful exegesis. The other side of the coin is uniformitarianism which, if accepted uncritically, nullifies much of the Old Testament, a significant amount of the world's ancient literature, and a great deal of Earth's geologic testimony.

If one accepts either or both of these erroneous assumptions, then he is required by the conflicting evidence to begin fabricating *ad hoc* explanations — a growing house of cards — in order to deal with his inconsistencies. He will also find it necessary to resort to seeming human logic, not the scripture and not the full natural evidence. Those principles which we consider axiomatic must be allowed to be challenged until they are firmly established, emended or disproven.

---

[7] Fields, *op. cit.*, p. 43.

[8] Skinner, *op. cit.*, p. 14, note. Several commentators who discuss the restitution hypothesis demonstrate its utter impossibility, e.g., Dillmann, Stigers, Allis. Hyers, *op. cit.*, p. 39, calls it "bizarre." Every Christian who has considered the gap theory to be plausible should read Fields' *Unformed and Unfilled, op. cit.*, for a complete and devastating critique.

The gap theory was formulated, as we have seen, because of an uncritical acceptance of two doubtful premises, a biblical traditionalism and the uniformitarian hypothesis. First, the correct exegesis of Gen. 1:1-3 utterly voids the gap theory: a billion-year gap in the middle of a sentence is incredible. Even assuming the traditional translation, the Bible contains not a shred of evidence for the gap theory. Second, there is the uniformitarian hypothesis requiring long ages, an idea that has made the gap theory appear necessary to some Christians. This is not the place to deal with the mountains of evidence that challenge the doctrine of uniformitarianism. Let us merely note that this philosophy has long been assumed but never demonstrated.

Thus the gap theory was unnecessary. Still worse, some of its proponents have asserted — again, according to a characteristic 19th century pietistic logic — that the angels' Fall took place during this "hiatus" between verses 1 and 2. The chaos of verse 2 is explained as the result of the angelic rebellion and casting down to Earth. Although the Bible gives us no hint of such a placement for the heavenly warfare (Gen. 6:2 may be a better potential "dating" for that "event"), yet there is one note of honesty to be found in the gap theory. Of all the alternative theories, it is one that takes seriously this fact: verse 1 speaks of an organized cosmos, while verse 2 describes a chaotic earth. But of course the gap theory, requiring numerous hairline-thin scriptural distinctions, is exegetically impossible.

A similar concordistic theory appeared in 1784. Francois Xavier Burtin proposed that the fossils demonstrated the ruins of the period he called "the chaos" *prior to* Day One of Genesis.[9] A more modern commentator, Merrill Unger, has proposed, in the middle of a carefully reasoned exegesis, the same hypothesis of at least one prior earth-age, destroyed by

---

[9] Haber, *op. cit.*, p. 152.

God, says Unger soberly, because of sin: "Thus Gen. 1:1,2 evidently describes not the primeval creation *ex nihilo*, celebrated by the angels (Job 38:7; Isaiah 45:18), but the much later refashioning of a judgment-ridden earth in preparation for a new order of creation — man."[10] Unger is determined to posit a re-creation whether or not the biblical context or science demands it. He does not realize how much he has been affected by modern rationalistic thinking; he need not portray a pre-biblical destruction of which the Bible says nothing and which geology and paleontology do not require. To his credit, however, Unger is attempting to swallow courageously the bitter pill of the pre-existent chaos of Gen. 1:2.

The most persuasive group of concordistic theories suggest that the seven-day sequence of Gen. 1:1 - 2:4 is merely a "literary framework" to glorify God as Creator, never to describe a literal calendar of the Creation. Many variations on the literary framework or day-age hypothesis have been proposed, and several of them are eloquent; but every one begins with man's wisdom and forces it upon the word of God. Such reinterpretations are a modern phenomenon; the ancients knew better.[11] In a variation today called "progressive creationism," each of the six days of creation becomes as long an "era" as modern rational man choses to make it. "Yet what the progressive creationist has done is to

---

[10] Merrill F. Unger, "Rethinking the Genesis Account of Creation," *op. cit.*, p. 28. E. J. Young (*op. cit.*) and Fields (*op. cit.*) both deal convincingly with interpretations such as Ungers', but they nowhere refute the thesis forming the basis of the present work.

[11] *Christianity Today*, *op. cit.*, p. 24, stated editorially that Augustine held to a form of the literary framework hypothesis, but this assertion has been thoroughly refuted by David C. C. Watson, *Bible Science Newsletter*, Vol. 22, No. 5, May 1984, pp. 1f.

turn Genesis 1 into a scientific allegory."[12]

Therefore any literary framework must deal first with the word "day" — *yom* in Hebrew. The word must be understood "figuratively," we are told. Although some biblical usages of "day" were clearly intended to express very limited periods of time, the day-age interpretation here is utterly invalid. Gen. 1 paints a clear picture, without question as to what the scripture means: "And there was evening and there was morning, one day,...a second day,...a third day, etc." Only by a willful attempt to twist the scripture could an exegete find anything but one earth-calendar-day, based upon Earth's rotation (not upon the sun, which appears on Day Four), in each of those sentences. Marcus Dods long ago dealt decisively with such a practice.

> The Bible needs no defense such as false constructions of its language bring to its aid. They are its worst friends who distort its words that they may yield a meaning more in accordance with scientific truth. If, for example, the word 'day' in these chapters does not mean a period of twenty-four hours, the interpretation [all exegesis] of scripture is hopeless.[13]

If any version of the literary framework theory is correct, then Gen. 1 must be incorrect! Its proponents may not legitimately claim to believe "the whole Bible."

Further, those Christians who would change "day" into "age" are not doing their homework in the Hebrew lexicons. A lexical study of *yom* demonstrates biblically that it never means a long, indeterminate age. But commentators promoting the literary framework theory do not reveal that fatal

---

[12] Hyers, *op. cit.*, p. 91.

[13] Dods, *The Book of Genesis*, The Expositor's Bible, N.Y.: A. C. Armstrong & Son, 1903, p. 4.

information when they tell us that *yom* must be interpreted figuratively.[14]

Yet Christian scholars opt for this hypothesis quite often. *Christianity Today*[15] presents an impassioned editorial appeal to impress a longer — much longer — meaning upon the word "day."[16] The editor would convince his readers that such is the way most evangelical scholars interpret Gen. 1.

Ridderbos asks, "Are we to take literally the representation that for every great work (or two works) of creation He used a day? It is open to serious doubt whether the author of Genesis 1, who proves to have such a sublime concept of God, actually meant to say that."[17] What is Ridderbos' textual basis for his "serious doubt"? His exegesis is open to serious doubt!

The Living Bible's paraphrasers committed a grievous error in their footnote to Gen. 1:8 (and elsewhere): "Literally, 'There was evening and there was morning, a second day (or, "period of time").'" Again, do they have a shred of textual evidence for inserting the optional "period of time"? Those words were clearly intended arbitrarily to legitimize the day-age hypothesis.[18] Even so strong a biblical inerrantist as Gleason Archer yields to scientistic pressure, giving the *yom* of Gen. 1 an indeterminate definition; he also favors the pre-

---

[14] Fields, *op. cit.*, details the evidence disproving the day-age interpretation, pp. 168f.

[15] *Christianity Today*, *op. cit.*, pp. 22f.

[16] For a detailed response see E. J. Young, *op. cit.*, pp. 43f. Young later comments pointedly on the literary framework hypothesis: "The basic reason why Moses used the device of six days was that creation occurred in six days." (p. 82, note).

[17] N. H. Ridderbos, *Is There a Conflict between Genesis 1 and Natural Science?*, Grand Rapids: Eerdmans, 1957, p. 31.

[18] *The Living Bible*, Wheaton, IL: Tyndale House, 1971, p. 1.

biblical ruin-and-re-creation model.[19] Archer needs to know that his attempts at harmonization are unnecessary and quite troublesome to the Church of Jesus Christ.

Obviously one who suggests such a forced, *ad hoc* meaning upon the days of Genesis 1 must already have accepted uncritically the idea of an old earth. In fact, gradualistic thinking is so deeply imbedded in his concept of origins that he would require scripture to be emended to fit his understanding of natural science.

> Among their writings one will *never* [italics added] find statements such as : "after years of study in the Hebrew text, and after comparing many grammars and lexicons as well as all of scriptural usage, we have finally come to the conclusion that the days of Genesis 1 *must* be interpreted, on the basis of its linguistic, grammatical, and syntactical features, as long periods of time, rather than normal, 24-hour days.[20]

The day-age theory derives then, not from careful Bible study, but from the scientistic attempt to harmonize Genesis with current scientific theory. This is often true even of one who claims to hold to biblical inerrancy. He perceives geological data through uniformitarian eyes. The universal, enormous signatures of the Flood remain misinterpreted. He will not question his basic assumptions. E. J. Young says of such a concordistic view,

> What strikes one immediately...is the low estimate of the Bible which it entails. Whenever science and the Bible are in conflict, it is always the Bible that, in one manner or another, must give way. We are not told that science should correct its answers in the light of Scripture... Yet this is really surprising, for the answers which scientists have provided have fre-

---

[19] Gleason Archer, *Encyclopedia of Bible Difficulties*, Grand Rapids: Zondervan, 1982, pp. 58-65.

[20] Fields, *op. cit.*, p. 166.

quently changed with the passing of time. The 'authoritative' answers of pre-Copernican scientists are no longer acceptable; nor, for that matter, are many of the views of twenty-five years ago.[21]

Once a progressive creationist begins harmonizing the Creation narrative with "modern science," he opens the door for another rationalistic re-interpretation. The "days" of Genesis 1 are obviously out of order, he thinks, so, to begin with, we must reverse Days Three and Four. After all, the sun was necessary for photosynthesis of the third day's green plants. This and other such attempts inevitably follow the first concordistic step. From that point theistic evolutionary thinking is but one gentle step.

An additional *ad hoc* theory is another that betrays the authenticity of scripture. Already noted above (see Exegesis of Gen. 1:1-3) is the group of commentators who desire to retain the traditional translation, but realize they must deal with the inherent contradiction of the chaos. So they state frankly that they feel that God created *tohu wabohu* — in spite of Genesis' silence and Isaiah's clear testimony to the contrary. This is a characteristic traditional interpretation. Again we find an attempt at honesty with the basic scripture, while violating the larger biblical context. John Diodati, a Reformed theologian living in Calvin's Geneva, gave his (and Calvin's) opinion in 1543:

> God giving the world its first being, began with the creation of the two general parts of it, and then went to the particulars... The lower and elementall part of the universe, here indifferently called earth, waters, and abysse, because it was a confused masse of all the Elements.[22]

---

[21] E. J. Young, *op. cit.*, p. 53.

[22] John Diodati, *Pious Annotations upon the Holy Bible*, London: Nicholas Fussell, 1543, p. 3.

As already noted, some prominent modern scholars are also to be found in this camp,[23] despite Child's assertion that

> It is rather generally acknowledged that the suggestion of God's first creating a chaos is a logical contradiction and must be rejected.[24]

Further, in Isaiah 45:18 the prophet asserts categorically, "He did not create it a *tohu!*"

To attribute the creation of the chaos of *tohu wabohu* in Gen. 1:2 to the God of the Bible is a serious error. In fact, the Hebrew words of verses 1 and 2 — "create" (*bara'*) and "chaos" (*tohu wabohu*) — are mutually exclusive and should not be used together, unless antithetically, as in Isaiah 45:18. Chaos throughout the Old Testament has an evil quality. Loretz says that chaos and creation are two absolute opposites. Creation, he states, consists of the ordering of chaos.[25] Loretz is correct; that is the biblical relationship of chaos and creation. Again it must be stated that in spite of the fact that a number of modern scholars — conservative and liberal — have credited God with the creation of the

---

[23] E.g., E. J. Young, *op. cit.*, says (p. 95): "The material from which the sun, moon and stars were made was created, i.e., brought into existence, at the absolute beginning [verse one]. On the fourth day God made of this primary material the sun and moon and stars... On the third day the creation of our globe was completed, although the primal material of the globe was brought into existence at the absolute beginning... Although the earth (i.e., in its original form) was created in the beginning, nevertheless, on Day three God made the earth." Young is obviously picking his way through a labyrinth of exegetical problems. Attempting to retain the axiomatic *ex nihilo*, he thus mars seriously an otherwise excellent presentation.

[24] Childs, *op. cit.*, p. 30.

[25] O. Loretz, *Schöpfung und Mythos*, Stuttgart: 1968, pp. 83f, noted in Hasel (*op. cit.*, p. 157), who as a traditionalist is quite unhappy with Loretz's proper exegesis.

chaos, it is highly unwarranted by the biblical context.[26] Von Rad insists, "To be sure, the notion of a created chaos is itself a contradiction."[27]   God is credited with creating everything else in Genesis 1, but no physical entity in verse 2, the "chaos" verse, is depicted as coming from his hand.

Some readers might consider this book to be merely another in a long line of concordistic theories, attempting once again to bridge a chasm between theology and geology. Not so! I was years ago aware of the Hebraic understanding of Gen. 1:1-3 because of a seminary course in Hebrew exegesis of the creation narratives. My interest in creationism developed later. Never since those seminary studies have I felt the need to search out a concordistic theory to explain away the obvious intent of these scriptures. My own experience has been one of distress over the stubborn adherence to the traditional translation and forced interpretations of Gen. 1:1-3 by otherwise competent creation scientists.

> We are happy where science confirms biblical statements, but contradictions cause us no consternation. To be sure, some such contradictions may be the result of improper biblical interpretation. If this is so, then the erroneous interpretations should be corrected. But let it never be forgotten: science is changing and the Bible is not. Therefore, what may be a contradiction now, may be completely resolved as science progresses. If we do not allow for the progress of science, we, too, may someday find ourselves left with neat harmonizations which no longer harmonize! Such a position cannot be legitimately criticized as "sticking one's head in the sand." It is not ignoring "the facts" — particularly ones dealing with dating — as any knowledge of scientific estimations of the earth's age

---

[26] Cf. Waltke, Part III, *op. cit.*, pp. 216-28.

[27] Von Rad, *op. cit.*, p. 46.

over the past one hundred years will show. Harmonizers ignore this.[28]

For several generations liberal Bible scholars on the Continent have provided the Christian world with some excellent Old Testament studies by dealing honestly with the scriptures exactly as they have found them — and in proper context. They are able to do this because they make no pretense of believing the entire Bible. In the English-speaking world, however, commentators often seem to have a deep urge to harmonize the Bible with the perceived natural world about them, thus burdening Christendom with some bizarre attempts at concord. So we may accept, for example, Gerhard von Rad's fine scholarship without adopting his personal world view. It is my opinion that von Rad is less dangerous to our faith than those seductive western writers who are the great harmonizers.

By this time my iconoclasm has surely succeeded in alienating every camp. Like the gentle young man who refused to identify with either side during the American Civil War — he wore a blue shirt and gray trousers and was shot by both armies — I must have irritated every reader at some point. However, this treatise has not been written to gather Establishment bouquets, whether from liberals or from creationists. I have been seeking only knowledge, which effort should hold a value in itself, trusting that the search has been fruitful. I trust too that the reader who has held to one or another of the concordistic theories is thankful to have been relieved of some of his lingering uneasiness by these revelations. To discover that neither Bible nor science need be forced should be quite liberating to a Christian.

---

[28] Fields, *op. cit.*, p. 46.

IX FROM CHAOS TO COSMOS

> [T]he theological thought of ch. 1 moves not so much
> between the poles of nothingness and creation as
> between the poles of chaos and cosmos.[1]

> Thus the text is interested directly in the gift of
> *form*, rather than the gift of *being*.[2]

Commentators who hold to the *creatio ex nihilo* position
in Gen. 1:1 often declare that those who disagree have a
problem: What is to be done about the chaos of verse 2?[3]
We have no problem with the chaos, for therein lies the
answer. The pre-Genesis scene so concisely pictured by the
biblical author is that of a primordial earth completely
covered with wild ocean waters and surrounded by a
darkened universe — a lonely, chaotic body, chosen by God
to be formed into something with order, beauty, light and
physical life.

Every western mind then asks the question, "But where
did that chaos come from?" Simply, the Bible doesn't say.[4]
The author of Gen. 1 is unconcerned about so rationalistic a
question.

> To the Greek the origin of matter was a pertinent and
> even pressing question. This is evidently not so with
> the [author of Gen. 1]. If he thought of the question at
> all, he was content to leave it unanswered. It is more

---

[1] Von Rad, *op. cit.*, p. 49.

[2] Blocher, *op. cit.*, p. 66.

[3] E.g., Hasel, *op. cit.*, p. 164.

[4] Cf. Waltke, Part IV, *op. cit.*, p. 338.

likely that it never entered his mind; he did not answer it because he was not aware of it as a question.[5]

What the Bible does portray so briefly in Gen. 1:1,2 is anticipatory of the God of order "seizing" co-existent protyle and forming a habitable planet, using the chaotic matter itself as the stuff of creation. The exposition of this "seizing," found largely in Job, Psalms and Isaiah, will be noted later.

The remainder of the first chapter (Gen. 1:3f) then describes the *process* of creation, the sequence of the various events. Eight major acts were compressed into those initial six days. The first four days were preparation and provision for the living beings; the final two days involved the actual creation of the animal kingdom and God's gift of *nephesh*, the quality of "living."

Tohu wabohu, that unformed chaos, to which are added the darkness and the watery deep, *tehom* — all are understood in Job, Psalms and several of the Prophets to have been dominated by entities which are at enmity with God. They are controlled by the "powers" resisting God's power.[6] God represents order, light, life, love, creation. The chaotic waters represents disorder, darkness, death, destruction. The bathic sea, the wild ocean waters, is that which was contained by God in the Creation.

---

[5] W. R. Lane, *op. cit.*, p. 73.

[6] Herman N. Gunkel in 1895 published his landmark *Schöpfung und Chaos in Urzeit und Endzeit* (Göttingen: Vanderhoeck und Ruprecht, 1895), depicting the cosmogonic warfare. Although flawed by typical late-19th century rationalistic logic, Gunkel's work contains a great deal of sound scholarship which should not be ignored. In recent years additional articles and books —

Parts of the Old Testament other than Genesis tell of that containment. "He gathered the waters of the sea as in a bottle; he put the deeps in storehouses" (Psalms 33:7). "The waters stood above the mountains. At thy rebuke they fled..." (Psalms 104:6b, 7a). "He assigned to the sea its limit, so that the waters might not transgress his command, when he marked out the foundations of the earth" (Prov. 8:29). "He...pushed the oceans back to let dry land appear" (Psalms 24:2, paraphrased in the Living Bible). The scene is one of all-out warfare.[7]

The warfare of Creation Week is not a struggle between equals. God is clearly superior, but Evil incarnate resists at every turn, as it does to this day. The Bible pictures a "leashing" of the primordial waters that the earth might be habitable for God's special creation in his own image, Man. God speaks through the prophet in Jer. 5:22b of how He restricted the threatening deep that completely surrounded the dry land: "I placed the sand as a bound for the sea, a

---

inspired by the archaeological finds at Ugarit — have been written about the theomachy. The Ugaritic literature has greatly helped to moderate Gunkel's excesses.

For the student interested in pursuing the subject further, see Mary K. Wakeman, *God's Battle with the Monster*, Leiden: E. J. Brill, 1973; Gordon, "Leviathan: Symbol of Evil," *op. cit.*, Nicholas K. Kiessling, "Antecedents of the Medieval Dragon in Sacred History," *Journal of Biblical Literature*, LXXXIX, 1970, pp. 167-77; Bernhard W. Anderson, *Creation versus Chaos*, N.Y.: Association Press, 1967; Marvin H. Pope, *Job*, and Mitchell J. Dahood, *Psalms I, II, III*, Anchor Bible, *op. cit.*

[7] Cardona, in "Creation and Destruction," (*op. cit.*, p. 73) says, "[*Bara'*] has the etymological meaning of 'forcing into shape.' The word also contains a connotation of violence."

perpetual barrier which it cannot pass; though the waves toss, they cannot prevail, though they roar, they cannot pass over it." Psalms 104:9 continues the same thought: "Thou didst set a bound which they should not pass, so that they might not again cover the earth."

The English word which most accurately describes this forceful action of God's Spirit upon the darkness and the waters is "muzzle," as one would muzzle a wild dog. Job 7:12 asks, in recalling the ancient tradition, "Am I the sea, or a sea monster, that you muzzle me?"[8] Job 38:8-11 describes an all-powerful God telling of his titanic feat of muzzling the rebellious powers:

> Or who shut in the sea with doors,
>   when it burst forth from the womb;
> when I made the clouds its garment,
>   and thick darkness its swaddling band;
> and prescribed bounds for it,
>   and set bars and doors,
> and said, 'Thus far shall you come, and no farther,
>   and here shall your proud waves be stayed'?

Based upon the Ugaritic (a Semitic dialect similar to Hebrew) Psalms 68:22 is emended to read, "I stifled the serpent; I muzzled the deep sea."[9] The apocryphal Prayer of Manasseh addresses God "...who hast shackled [muzzled] the sea by thy word of command, who hast confined the deep..." (v. 3). It is quite interesting to note that Jesus of Nazareth, recalling those primeval events in which He had Himself participated, spoke authoritatively when confronted once again by the darkness and wild waters on the Sea of Galilee: "He...rebuked the wind, and said to the sea, 'Be muzzled!'" (Gk. *pephimoso*; Mark 4:39a). This expression was charac-

---

[8] Mitchell J. Dahood, "Mišmār 'Muzzle' in Job 7:12," *Journal of Biblical Literature and Exegesis*, 80, 1961, pp. 271-72. Cf. Pope, *Job*, Anchor Bible, *op. cit.*, pp. 60, 61.

[9] *Ibid.*, pp. 271-72.

teristic of the various ancient Mesopotamian and Canaanite literatures; Albright translates a Ugaritic inscription, "I muzzled Tannin [the Dragon]..."[10]

Significant too is the watery source of five apocalyptic beasts, "four great beasts" of Daniel 7:3 who "came up out of the sea," and Revelation's beast who was seen "...rising out of the sea..." (13:1a). In apocalyptic symbolism the sea usually represents the peoples of the world (at enmity with God), e.g., Rev. 17:15. The LXX translators rendered *tehom* as *abyssos,* later to be found in the New Testament as the abyss, the abode of the unrighteous dead. For an Old Testament precedent, see Psalms 71:20, where *tehom* in the plural has just such a meaning.[11]

Job 26:12 continues in even more shocking (to the modern mind) language the portrayal of the battle of creation: "By his power he stilled the sea; by his understanding he smote Rahab... His hand pierced the fleeing serpent." And so Isaiah, "Was it not thou that didst cut Rahab in pieces, that didst pierce the dragon?" (51:9b). The coiled, evasive serpent, in the Bible variously given the appellatives Rahab, Leviathan, the dragon, is the personification of, or analogous to, the evil which has been restricted by God in the Creation. The evil forces resisting the Creator are consistently linked to the sea, the deep, the wild ocean waters. [12] [13] In fact, all the Old Testament descriptions of

[10] William F. Albright, in the *Bulletin of the American Schools of Oriental Research*, No. 84, 1941, p. 16; quoted in Alexander Heidel, *op. cit.*, p. 106.

[11] Cf. Howard Wallace, "Leviathan and the Beast in Revelation," *The Biblical Archaeologist*, Vol. XI, No. 3, Sept. 1948, pp. 66-67.

[12] Wakeman, *op. cit.*, p. 102: The sea (*yam*) "is found parallel to...Rahab. Leviathan and the tannin [dragon], as well as to *tehom*." Additional Old Testament references to the anti-creation serpent/waters are Job 3:8; 9:13; 41:1f; Psalms 89:9,10; 93:3,4; 104:25,26; Hab. 3:8-15.

[13] Jacob, *op. cit.*, p. 141: "It is not without reason that the Israelites

God's struggle and victory over Rahab-Leviathan-dragon-*tehom*-darkness, except where used metaphorically, *always* refer back to the Creation.[14]

Waltke says that these Old Testament poetic references, so similar to the seven-headed monster of the ancient Near Eastern creation myths, merely "served as a helpful metaphor to describe Yahweh's creative activity"[15] for the authors of Job, Psalms and Isaiah. In other words, Waltke suggests that strict monotheists could never have believed those stories literally, as did all their pagan neighbors. Such myths were "borrowed imagery," used only poetically, therefore not to be taken seriously.

Yet Waltke (and other conservative scholars who also believe in biblical inerrancy) should be asked if he believes the re-telling of the seven-headed dragon story that appears so prominently in Rev. 12, or the seven-headed beast of Rev. 13. In summary, can we legitimately consider Old Testament theomachies as metaphors, similes or myths, yet treat the more up-to-date New Testament references with considerably more reverence? Such conclusions could be considered to be inconsistent exegesis, probably attributable to our modern rationalistic world view.

There *are* certain genuine metaphorical uses of Rahab, the dragon/serpent, in the Old Testament. These allegorical nicknames are always carefully noted as referring to the earthly enemies of God and his people (e.g., Psalms 40:4 ["the proud"]; 87:4; Isaiah 30:7; Jeremiah 51:34; Ezekiel 29:3; 32:2). We find such a metaphorical use even as late as the

---

did not become a seafaring people and that they always showed a kind of instinctive horror of the sea and its dangers."

[14] Wakeman, *op. cit.*, p. 3.

[15] Waltke, Part I, *op. cit.*, p. 34.

pseudepigraphal Psalms of Solomon (2:29) in the 1st century B.C., where the author speaks disparagingly of the Roman conqueror of Palestine, Pompey. Early Christian polemics maintain this same imagery concerning their earthly enemies.[16] However, the instances of metaphor are easily perceived by their contexts. All other Old Testament references to Rahab, Leviathan, the dragon/serpent, speak specifically of the archenemy of God's Creation. The biblical writers possessed a strong anti-mythological bias, giving us all the more reason for dealing with this material more than casually.

The Old Testament monster too is multi-headed: "You shattered the heads of the dragon[17] on the waters; you crushed the heads of Leviathan" (Psalms 74:13b,14a). Ancient Mesopotamian and Canaanite myths all tell us this anti-creation dragon has seven heads; from Ugarit comes this inscription:

> When thou shalt smite Lotan, the fleeing serpent,
> (And) shalt put an end to the tortuous serpent,
> Shalyat of the seven heads...[18]

Revelation confirms the ancient memory with its seven-headed dragon (12:3) and seven-headed "beast rising out of the sea" (13:1).

Both Testaments speak clearly of incarnate evil having been decisively defeated by God, merely restricted for the present, but both anticipate the final destruction and

---

[16] Kiessling, *op. cit.*, pp. 172f.

[17] See Wakeman, *op. cit.*, pp. 63, 68, note 5, where "dragons" or, "sea monsters" [*tanninim*], is to be translated in the singular. The plural of the Masoretic text violates the original Hebrew parallelism. Cf. Kittel, *Biblia Hebraica*, p. 1040, note to v. 13.

[18] Heidel, *op. cit.*, p. 107.

disposition of Earth's enemy at a future time.[19]

> Leviathan...is a monster who sums up cosmic evil and
> was vanquished by God of old and will be annihilated
> by God once and for all in the end of days.[20]

Isaiah 27:1 foretells this eschatological event.

> In that day the Lord with his hard and great and
> strong sword will punish Leviathan the fleeing serpent,
> Leviathan the twisting serpent, and he will slay the
> dragon that is in the sea.

Leviathan is consistently linked to the sea (and Job's
Behemoth to the land). John of Patmos knew very well the
Old Testament imagery of the multi-headed beast of *tehom*;
thus Revelation concludes the theomachy with that gentle
statement of ultimate triumph: "...and the sea was no
more" (21:1).

The "personality" of the evil chaos is evident in scripture.
Indeed, the Hebrew *tehom* — "the deep" — appears to be a
proper name; as with any proper name there is rarely an
article ("the") before it; thus a strictly literal translation
would be "Deep" rather than "the deep."[21] There is no word
or concept in biblical Hebrew for an impersonal "nature." *All*
sources are spiritual, personal. Nothing "just happens"; there
is divine activity — good or evil — behind every earthly
event. Read Job 1 and 2 with this in mind. Water itself is not
that which is evil, but rather the malevolent spiritual power
controlling the seas. Indeed, water in the creation narrative

---

[19] Apparently the future elimination of the dragon/waters was
common currency in 1st century Judaism, appearing in the
pseudepigraphal Testament of Levi 4:1 and Assumption of
Moses 10:6.

[20] Gordon, "Leviathan: Symbol of Evil," *op. cit.*, p. 9. Cf. G. C. D.
Howley, F. F. Bruce, H. L. Ellison, eds., *The New Laymen's
Bible Commentary,* Grand Rapids: Zondervan, 1979, p. 135.

[21] Wakeman, *op. cit.*, p. 89.

of Gen. 2 is the very basis for fertility. The ocean and the fresh water are contrasted, one misused by a hostile spiritual power and the other used by a caring God as a life-giving necessity.

"And God saw that it was good..." contrasts the nature of the newly formed earth with the evil chaos that had formerly been reigning unchained. The Hebrew word for "good" has a broader range than its English translation; "very good" could well be chosen to capture the fullness of intent.[22] In fact, Gen. 1:31 looks back at the Creation, describing it in much stronger terms, "and God saw everything that he had made, and behold, it was *very* good." So, if we use "very good" above, perhaps better in verse 31 would be "extremely good"!

Because God's "goodness" is aligned against the evil powers of chaos, there is actually a severe struggle occurring. God is always superior, but the evil powers never quit fighting. The natural events that were taking place must have been awesome. The ocean bottoms were heaving up to expose the ground, probably a single land mass ("Pangaea"), for there is no biblical indication of separate continents until "...the earth was divided" (Gen. 10:25). Thus the scripture, if this verse does indeed refer to the breakup of Pangaea, casually anticipates the modern theory of plate tectonics. In this massive upheaval described so concisely in verses 9 and 10, God was forming a place fit for habitation by his physical creations, both animal and plant life.

God firmly took charge in this spiritual warfare, with his Spirit "sweeping" across the rebellious waters and driving back the darkness with his light.[23] When God who is Spirit

---

[22] Ridderbos, *op. cit.*, p. 66; Speiser, *op. cit.*, p. 5.

[23] Jesus consistently portrayed the darkness as evil: "But this is your hour, and the power of darkness" (Luke 22:53b); "And cast the

speaks the word, no other power can prevent the results from occurring in the physical realm. The consummation of the opening round of the struggle perhaps has been noted quietly in verse 5: "...and the darkness he called Night." Historically, when one person forcibly took authority over another, the former normally seized the opportunity to "name" the vanquished.[24] The naming simply means that God had now established his authority over the darkness, although the darkness was permitted a limited nocturnal sovereignty.

God's first act of creation was to form light. Light is essential if Good is to prevail. In the Bible, light and darkness are separate, distinct entities,[25] in this present age inter-mingled, each one allowed to rule over its designated segment of the daily cycle, as depicted in Jer. 33:20: "Thus says the LORD: If you can break my covenant with the day and my covenant with the night, so that day and night will not come at their appointed time..."

"Order" and "history" belong together. God creates history; He begins by working through "...evening and morning, one day." Thus the Bible, from its very beginning, assumes a plan, a purpose, to history. Karl Barth says, "The aim of creation is history."[26] Chaos is non-historical; cosmos implies history. History, according to the Bible, is going somewhere.

And God keeps it going somewhere. The ancient Israelite perceived God's *sustaining* hand in the twice-daily tides, annual seasonal and river changes and each new day,

---

worthless servant into the outer darkness; there men will weep and gnash their teeth" (Matt. 25:30).

[24] Cf. E. J. Young, *op. cit.*, p. 35, note.

[25] Childs, *op. cit.*, p. 33. See Job 38:17,19.

[26] Karl Barth, *Church Dogmatics*, Vol. III, part I, Edinburgh: T. & T. Clark, 1958, p. 33.

new moon, new year. The earth is organized, but requires the Divine Sustainer. The chaos is not yet destroyed, only contained, co-existing with the order and life impressed upon the earth by God. The tension remains yet. Though the waters try to inundate, to regain their former supremacy, God is the Sustainer who prevents such a disaster, "...upholding the universe by his word of power" (Heb. 1:3a). Each morning He calls back the darkness (*choshek*); at every high tide He calls back *tehom*. Von Rad notes tersely, "The cosmos stands permanently in need of this supporting Creator's will."[27] Jacob describes the situation well.

> This direct intervention of God in nature is not only a proof of the lordship with which he makes use of all the elements; it sometimes takes the form of a veritable struggle, because in spite of its perfection, Creation is unceasingly menaced by two forces which have not been created by Yahweh but have simply been subjected to Him, namely darkness and the sea, residues of the chaos which existed before Creation. Darkness is a power hostile to Yahweh, whose essence is light... The sea constitutes a still graver menace... The vast domain of waters was...only more or less neutralized by being confined within certain limits assigned to them... But the water, though driven back, has only one desire, to return and take up again the place it originally occupied.[28]

> The raging, unruly waters of chaos symbolize the powers which threaten to destroy the meaningfulness of history, as though — to recall Jeremiah's vision — the world ever has the possibility of returning to chaos (Jer. 4:23-26).[29]

---

[27] Von Rad, *op. cit.*, p. 49; Bernhard W. Anderson, "The Earth Is the Lord's," *Interpretation*, Vol. IX, 1955, pp. 10-14, provides a grand statement about God the Sustainer.

[28] Jacob, *op. cit.*, p. 140.

[29] Anderson, *Creation versus Chaos*, *op. cit.*, p. 132.

Yet, if creation is an historical event, contrariwise, history is a continuation of this creative power of God. [Isaiah and Jeremiah] use such terms as [*'asah* and *yatsar*] in describing God's intervention in Hebrew history. Through the events of history, therefore, Yahweh is forming, making or creating history... At each moment of time, darkness must be dispelled and the raging waters of the abyss kept in their place by the creative word of God.[30]

Since God is the Creator, He retains the right to allow the earth to revert to its former state, which He accomplished temporarily in the Flood simply by removing his sustaining power. "The waters above" thereupon collapsed upon the earth during a 40-day period,[31] this catastrophe occurring simultaneously as "...all the fountains of the great deep burst forth" (Gen. 7:11). These worldwide eruptions didn't "just happen": God ordered them! *Baqa'* ("burst forth") in the present usage (simple passive form) means "a breaking forth (in order to liberate) *caused by* something or someone." These simultaneous events were probably what occasioned the end of the Paleozoic Era as arbitrarily designated on the uniformitarian geologic time scale. The entire creation — so beautiful and good in the beginning — sank to a much lower level of existence. Entropy set in with a vengeance, and sin-ridden man became the saddest specimen in all of God's handiwork.

God had declared man to be his deputy immediately upon the latter's creation in Gen. 1:26f. Man's responsibility on this earth was to "...fill the earth and subdue it." In his edenic setting man was assigned to be God's agent for controlling, for good, "...every living thing that moves upon

---

[30] Stuhlmueller, *op. cit.*, pp. 435, 465.

[31] A similar event occurred on a much smaller scale when "...the Lord brought back the waters of the [Red] Sea" to inundate the Egyptians pursuing Israel (Exodus 15:19).

the earth." After the Fall the image of God was marred by sin and death. Man has since tried to set himself up as sovereign, which in his sinful condition is only presumption. Being unable to effect this attempt at sovereignty, man usually finds himself tragically adding to the earth's disorder in the ages-long war between Good and Evil. A commentary on the Book of Revelation describes the situation well.

> There is a kind of reversal in [Revelation's] bowls of judgment of the process of creation, beginning with the earth, the sea, the sun, and ending with the general chaos of the whole ordered system of the world. The highly colored apocalyptic language thus represents a deep truth — that when men defy God, they are turning the world back into chaos.[32]

> Sin involves the danger of undermining the integrity of the Creation and of leading to a return of chaos.[33]

The natural principle involved here is called "entropy," a result of the Second Law of Thermodynamics.

Albert Einstein declared that entropy is the premier law of all science,[34] as Paul confirms in Romans 8:20-22: "...the creation was subjected to futility; ...the creation itself will be set free from its bondage to decay..." The Apostle proclaimed a principle in harmony with the Second Law of Thermodynamics 18 centuries before "natural" man could formalize it.

Wherever the Gospel is preached and heeded, however, increased "order" inevitably results. God's Spirit still today

---

[32] Herbert H. Wernecke, *The Book of Revelation Speaks to Us*, Philadelphia: Westminster Press, 1954, p. 130. Other reversals of the creation pattern have been noted elsewhere in scripture. Cf. Michael Fishbane, "Jeremiah IV 23-26 and Job III 3-13: A Recovered Use of the Creation Pattern,"*Vestus Testamentum*, Vol. XXI, 1971, pp. 151-67.

[33] Jacob, *op. cit.*, p. 141.

[34] Jeremy Rifkin, with Ted Howard, *Entropy: a New World View*, N.Y.: Viking Press, 1980, p. 6.

slows and even miraculously reverses the world's natural
entropy as Christians pray and believe Him.

> The spiritual plane is not governed by the ironclad
> dictates of the Entropy Law... While the Entropy Law
> governs the world of time, space, and matter, it is, in
> turn, governed by the primordial spiritual force that
> conceived it.[35]

Just as the Israelites' clothing did not wear out in 40 years in
the wilderness (Deut. 8:4), so is the final verse of the Gospel
of Mark true to this day: "They went forth and preached
everywhere, while the Lord worked with them and confirmed
the message by the miracles that attended it" (16:20). Miracles
are often dramatic, abrupt reversals of the world's natural
entropy.   In biblical language, they are demonstrations of
God's "saving" actions. Nations, communities, families and
individuals that are led by the Spirit of God soon begin to
witness noticeable slowings of entropy's "normal" rate of
degeneration. "Creation and salvation are almost identical
terms in the Old Testament."[36]

But, for all his frantic efforts, unspiritual, natural man is
more of a pawn in this universal struggle than he will admit.
His initial responsibility in this age is to choose sides — and
to lead others to choose sides — for the final conflict.

The Bible pictures *three stages* in this cosmic warfare
between God and chaos for control of the earth. The first
picture we see is that scene in Gen. 1:1,2 where chaos has full
sway. Verse 3 initiates what we could call the present age,
where order and chaos exist side-by-side, temporary
supremacy going now to one and now to the other, in a
centuries-long pattern of continuing warfare, although the
decisive battle has long since been fought at Calvary. This age
encompasses nearly all of scripture. The third, fulfillment

---

[35] *Ibid.*, p. 8.

[36] Boman, *op. cit.*, p. 182.

stage is described in the final two chapters of the Bible: "Then I saw a new heaven and a new earth; for the first heaven and the first earth had passed away, and the sea was no more." That last clause is more than an afterthought; it depicts a new earth where chaos is utterly nonexistent. Amos 7:4 predicts the final struggle in characteristic Old Testament language: "The Lord God was calling for judgment by fire, and it devoured the great deep [*tehom*]." "And there shall be continuous day" (Zech. 14:7a); "night shall be no more" (Rev. 22:5a). The chaos and the darkness are eliminated upon the conclusion of the war; the victory of Good is complete, and Evil is no longer merely chained but permanently cast into the flames.

Note once again that this new earth is not *creatio ex nihilo*. According to 2 Peter 3:5f, *fire* is God's primary instrument for destroying the present earth, but the new earth will be, in modern terms, the same earth — reformed, renewed, re-created — no longer oppressed by the old serpent-enemy, Satan. The Bible, as we can see, has a sublime, over-arching view of Earth's history, far more awesome and worship-inspiring than the pagan evolutionary theory of origins.

"Thus the heavens and the earth were finished, and all the host of them." So the scripture sums up the initial accomplishment, God's work of creation, from chaos to cosmos.

Why? WHERE? when? Who? What? If? Which? HOW MUCH?

QUESTIONS

1. WHEN DID THE "CREATION" OCCUR?

Surely every Christian who holds such a belief would like to conserve his theological "axiom" that God created the universe *ex nihilo*. Agreeing with the early 5th century Augustine, my own personal opinion is that God did just that — *but prior to Gen. 1:1!* I think so; but that is all. I am not nearly as certain of *creatio ex nihilo* as I am certain of those doctrines that the Bible clearly enunciates. Theological speculation can lead one astray — dangerously.

The questioning reader, now having noted my own (Augustinian) opinion of an original *pre-biblical* creation out of nothing, might wonder then why this book was written. First, and most important, I am convinced that the Bible speaks of a recent creation out of existing matter; Christians can understand the mighty biblical acts of God better with that knowledge. And second, there are ample scientific evidences of a very ancient lifeless earth and universe — which contradiction leads to confusion among creationists and loss of credibility in the scientific world. This work simply brings together data relating to the age of the earth from the two broad disciplines, with the delightful result that they could well be found to be in basic accord. Thus our study should prove helpful to scientists and Bible students alike, serving to relieve unnecessary tensions and disagreements.

To return to our subject, however, Rev. 21 and 22 raise a sobering question. Since those two chapters suggest a *future* eternity of matter, what does that say to our theories of origins? Do these final scriptures imply a past eternity of matter as well? We have no certain answer.

Let's ponder this question of *ex nihilo*. The point is not that God could not — or did not — create the universe from nothing. Rather, what is at issue is:

(1) Does any scripture *say* He created *ex nihilo* at that point in Gen. 1 where "history" begins? This question has surely been answered satisfactorily earlier.

(2) Is it appropriate to suggest that God created chaos (*tohu wabohu et al.*) when Isaiah 45:18 clearly states, "He did not create it a chaos [*tohu*]"? This question too has been examined.

Therefore, when did the "Creation" occur?

First, biblical chronology indicates that the Creation described in Gen. 1 occurred only a few thousand years ago. The entire half-billion-year-plus geologic column is telescoped by the Bible to within those few millennia. Although Genesis begins with this recent Creation, the Bible does speak elsewhere of several earlier "events."

> The Lord created [wisdom] at the beginning of his work, the first of his acts of old,... at the first, before the beginning of the earth, when there were no depths,... before he had made the earth... (Prov. 8:22f).

All the host of heaven [angels] was created prior to Gen. 1, "...for in [Chist] all things were created, in heaven and on earth, visible and invisible..." (Col. 1:16a). "All things were made through him" (John 1:3a). "When [God] laid the foundation of the earth,... all the sons of God [the heavenly host] shouted for joy" (Job 38:4a,7b). "[T]he book of life of the Lamb that was slain" contains names that were "...written before the foundation of the world..." (Eph. 1:4; Rev. 13:8b). Perhaps Behemoth could even be included: "He is the first of the works [or, ways] of God" (Job 40:19), if Behemoth here is perceived as a primordial being of spiritual nature, as Leviathan is usually understood.

Of these prior "events" we are told in scripture, but of the pre-biblical origins of Earth, of *tehom*, *choshek* and *tohu wabohu* we are told nothing.[1] Even the angels' Fall is not definitely placed, although it may have been recorded in a later context for good reason (Gen. 6:2); the pseudepigraphal Book of Jubilees and Book of Enoch both seem to confirm this view.

One might ask, logically, How then did a proposed *creatio ex nihilo* — whenever it took place — come to be controlled by rebellious powers, since according to Isaiah God did not create a chaos?

First, Isaiah refers only to the Creation of Gen. 1 as not being a chaos (uninhabitable); the author never speaks of an earlier, hypothetical creation out of nothing. Second, we have no biblical evidence for dating a proposed pre-Adamic Fall of the angels, so these rationalistic ponderings about the chaos are perhaps only a modern "busy-ness." Time and matter are inseparable; an angelic "rebellion" would have occurred, not in time, but in eternity. One can perceive easily why some very modern commentators have posited a pre-Genesis Fall. But the presence in the world of pre-creation Evil has no necessary identity with the (later?) Fall of the angels. The question may be unanswerable on this side of heaven.

---

[1] The 11th century Rashi makes an interesting observation about *tehom*.

> And if you should say that (the verse) comes to teach that these (heaven and earth) were created first, and that its interpretation is: In the beginning of every thing (first of all) He created these... — in that case (if you insist that the passage -indicates the order of Creation), you should be astonished at yourself, for indeed, the waters came first,... and as yet Scripture had not revealed, when the creation of the waters took place. (From) this you learn that the waters came before the earth [the dry land]...Scripture does not teach us anything about the order of the earlier or later (acts of creation). (Rashi, *op. cit.*, pp. 2,3).

But when did the "original" Creation occur?

The question worded in this manner means *creatio ex nihilo*, whenever and however it might have occurred, assuming of course that matter is not eternal. The Bible nowhere speaks of such an "event," much less provide a dating of absolute creation out of nothing. This work avoids speculation about such matters where the Bible could speak but remains silent.

Scientific conjectures are safer. For example, if the big-bang theory could overcome its *scientific* challenges, that date for the "original" Creation might have been ten billion-or-more years ago. But, without some crucial emendation, even the big-bang could not accommodate creation out of nothing!

More promising is the newer concept of the "inflationary universe." The already traditional big-bang theory cannot explain what might have happened during the first few moments of creation, specifically, the initial second. And theoretical physicists are challenging the big-bang theory on additional grounds. A new unified field theory, drawing together all the basic forces of the universe, fits elegantly into a creationist scenario of *creatio ex nihilo* — 10 to 15 billion years ago! — and quite compatibly with the primary thesis of this book. The model of the inflationary universe seems to agree

> with the generally accepted description of the observed universe for all times after the first 10^{-30} second... According to the inflationary model, the universe had

---

As noted earlier, Psalms 104:6a might be referring to the Creation-event: "Thou didst cover [the earth] with *tehom* as with a garment." Some feel however that this verse refers to the Flood.

Charles notes a later rabbinic tradition: "...seven things created before the world,... Torah, Repentance, the Garden of Eden, Gehenna, the Throne of Glory, the Temple, and the Messiah..." (R. H. Charles, *Pseudepigrapha*, Oxford: Clarendon Press, 1913, p. 562, note).

> a brief period of rapid inflation, or expansion... In the course of this stupendous growth spurt all the matter and energy in the universe could have been created from virtually nothing.[2]

The model of the inflationary universe not only appears to explain and predict accurately many observed characteristics of the universe, but it also leads to those startling final words. Guth and Steinhardt conclude their article with this plausibly prophetic statement:

> The inflationary model of the universe provides a possible mechanism by which the observed universe could have evolved from an infinitesimal region. It is then tempting to go one step further and speculate that *the entire universe evolved from literally nothing.*[3] [italics added].

Whether or not this theory is correct will remain for future research to ascertain, but it certainly harmonizes quite well with all that has been said about creation in this book.

The Second Law of Thermodynamics—entropy—also suggests some sort of initial creation. The world is "running down"; thus logic would appear to require that it have had a beginning, and, because the universe is yet far from equilibrium, it must have begun in the not-too-distant past. This *seems* to be appropriate.

Dating the recent formation of the earth (and the heavens) from pre-existing material as noted in Gen. 1:2 is as far back as we can proceed *biblically* without stumbling in the darkness. Perhaps Bishop Ussher was not correct about the date of the Creation, but he was much closer than Charles Lyell's arbitrary uniformitarianism. Because of the discrepancies between the ancient manuscripts and versions, Creation Week is often estimated biblically to have occurred six to eight thousand years ago. Many creationists feel

---

[2] Alan H. Guth & Paul J. Steinhardt, "The Inflationary Universe," *Scientific American*, Vol. 250, No. 5, May 1984, p. 116.

[3] *Ibid.*, p. 128.

compelled to add several more millennia. That opinion seems reasonable; the great variation of centuries between the ancient versions of Genesis appears to make it a possibility. The most plausible figures — scripturally — are in the thousands, certainly not billions of years. The mounting *natural* evidence in our own generation, combined with the correct exegesis of Gen. 1, makes so recent a dating no longer appear ridiculous to the open-minded inquirer.

One simple illustration. The Lompoc, California, diatomaceous earth beds are organic deposits of a type that is said to be building at the rate of one to five centimeters per thousand years.[4] These figures for the deposition of the thick diatomite deposits are then extrapolated to many millions of years by uniformitarian logic, and this intimidating "evidence" is presented to prove the concept of long ages for life on the earth.[5] Herein is seen an example of old Earth advocates' only strong argument for very ancient life — sedimentary deposits containing once-living organisms in extremely thick strata. Implicit within this argument is also to be found gradualism's greatest weakness — its basic, unquestioned *assumption* that these deposits have always accumulated at rates not very much different from those which are current. The *rate* of processes is the controversial point.

It is fortunate for scientific inquiry that diatomaceous earth has commercial value, for in 1976 in the quarry at Lompoc workers uncovered an 80-foot-long baleen whale —

---

[4] Arthur N. Strahler, *Physical Geology*, N.Y.: Harper & Row, 1981, p. 243.

[5] Daniel Wonderly, "Non-radiometric Data Relevant to the Question of Age," *Journal of the American Scientific Affiliation*, Vol. 27, No. 4, Dec. 1975, p. 147; D. Young, *op. cit.*, pp. 78f.

standing on its tail![6]

Obviously the whale *and* the diatomite were all thrust into that pit *catastrophically*, and in minutes instead of millennia. Actually, the whale had been lying on its side: the entire deposit had then been turned violently into its present position 90 degrees from its original orientation. Suddenly the burden of proof shifts. This single striking discovery of "a whale on its tail" renders utterly invalid any uniformitarian use of the Lompoc beds as evidence for ages older than biblical chronology allows, and it certainly strengthens the case for flood geology. Surely also this discovery should initiate some caution among old earth adherents as they retroject current rates of all other organic depositions into the "prehistoric" past. Apart from the commercial value of the Lompoc diatomite, these beds would continue to be used improperly as evidence for an old earth.

Gradualists today will generally admit to "local" catastrophes, such as earthquakes, vulcanism, and, of course, a more widespread Ice Age. But the "glasses" they wear cannot seem to admit the possibility of worldwide catastrophes, at least in recent millennia. Indeed, the scope of such a global event as the Flood would have been so enormous as to be incredible to the modern geologist who, perhaps, cannot see the forest for the trees.

---

[6] *Chemical & Engineering News*, Oct. 11, 1976, p. 40.

2. WHAT DID GOD INTEND BY GENESIS 1:1-3?

The initial chapter of Genesis bears another distinctive quality that has not yet been noted. It should be observed first that many of the narrative portions of the Old Testament are written in non-chronological order, e.g., Gen. 2.[1] The precise order of events is often not a concern of the biblical writer. Gen. 1, on the other hand, is a revelation from God that bears all the marks of precise sequence, with a unique concern (among the ancient Hebrews) for "time" in a language whose "tenses" are based upon the state of an action, not time of occurrence. Von Rad says it best.

> Nothing is here by chance; everything must be considered carefully, deliberately, and precisely... What is said here is intended to hold true entirely and exactly as it stands. There is no trace of the hymnic element in the language, nor is anything said that needs to be understood symbolically or whose deeper meaning has to be deciphered... These sentences cannot easily be overinterpreted theologically! Indeed, to us the danger appears greater that the expositor will fall short of discovering the concentrated doctrinal context.[2]

God is speaking clearly and distinctly in chapter 1. If the chapter is exegeted properly, it will be discovered that He provides a wealth of understanding of immense value to every generation of mankind.

But let's limit our present concern to the first three verses. It has already been ascertained what the *author* meant

---

[1] E. J. Young, *op. cit.*, pp. 74-76.

[2] Von Rad, *op. cit.*, pp. 47, 48. Heidel, *op. cit.*, insists however that Gen. 1:27,28 "are poetry pure and simple. The whole chapter is written in a solemn tone and in dignified prose...which easily glides over into poetry" (p. 93, note). While the earlier portion of his assertion may be true, Heidel's final six words strain our credulity.

by these opening lines. Now we need to ask further, What did *God* intend by those words?

It may be found elsewhere in scripture that God sometimes adds a subsequent, "ultimate" meaning to particular scriptures.[3] Did He perhaps attach further meaning to Gen. 1:1-3 for latter-day readers? Until we examined more carefully the creation references of Romans 4:17 and Hebrews 11:3, God *appeared* to have added *ex nihilo* to Genesis' creation narratives. This possibility should have been reconsidered already by the reader who is not bound by religious tradition. The doctrine of creation has been clearly demonstrated not to be an example of what is called progressive revelation. In the New Testament, particularly in 2 Peter and Revelation, creation still means what it meant in the Old Testament; for the Apostle Paul and the author of Hebrews a Platonic philosophical quality has been added.

The Bible fairly shouts that God is consistent. If He is going to alter his course or accomplish a unique work, God always alerts his servants the prophets (Amos 3:7). Otherwise He does not vary, "for I the Lord do not change" (Mal. 3:6). To illustrate, let's examine his pattern concerning creative miracles all through the scripture. Every formation of life recorded in Gen. 1 and 2 was just that — a creative miracle.

The Lord is not limited by the First Law of Thermodynamics (conservation of energy). Christians believe that

---

[3] Cf. Conrad E. L'Heureux, "Understanding the Old Testament Prophecies," *The Bible Today*, Vol. 23, No. 1, Jan. 1985, pp. 56-57; Ridderbos, *op. cit.*, p. 18. E.g., Matthew 2:15: "Therefore was fulfilled what was spoken by the prophet, 'Out of Egypt have I called my son.'" That New Testament verse refers to the angelic instruction to Joseph to return home from Egypt with his infant Son Jesus. But as we look back to Hosea 11:1b, we find that the original statement referred to Israel's exodus out of Egypt under Moses. God gave Hosea's statement additional, "ultimate" meaning in the New Testament. Such a "dual fulfillment" is quite common in biblical prophecy.

God could create out of nothing any time He desires. The biblical record provides consistent evidence, however, that He does not. All creative miracles in the Bible begin with at least a "seed."

In Gen. 2:7 the LORD God formed man from the ground; in verses 21 and 22 He took one of the man's ribs to "build up" a woman. The Sidonian widow offered Elijah only a handful of meal and a little oil, yet the food lasted for more than two years (1 Kings 17:16). Elisha prayed for the widow of his student-prophet and God multiplied her tiny supply of oil (2 Kings 4:1-7). Note that in each case God began to create with something "in hand."

Jesus of Nazareth never performed a creative miracle out of nothing. He placed mud or spit on damaged eyeballs to produce two complete eyes. He made wine out of water. He fed 5,000 with five loaves of bread and two fish. In Matt. 15:30,31 people with missing hands or feet found to their joy that new ones had grown out of the stumps. God's miracles always seem to have some material to begin with. Not that the Almighty Creator *needs* material, but rather, He appears to have chosen to limit Himself so that He regularly creates in such a manner. So consistent a *modus operandi* indicates the process by which God in Gen. 1 created the earth as well. The very laws under which He operates today are the same laws operative in the Creation of Gen. 1.

The Book of Isaiah, for example, portrays the predicted re-establishment of the nation of Judah following the Babylonian exile in specific terms of *creation*. The author repeatedly relates the formation of the heavens and the earth to the coming re-creation of the Jewish nation, using *bara'*, *'asah* and *yatsar* freely and interchangeably. Thus creation identical in terms and concept appears in both Genesis and Isaiah. "This historical act of re-creating Israel unveils God's power in creating the universe out of primal chaos."[4] The final two chapters of Revelation also speak of re-creation in much the same manner.

> God's creative activity is thus not limited to the genesis of the world, *as it is for us*, but creation is a collective concept which expresses all the positive saving actions of God at all times...[5] [italics added]

Boman clearly recognizes our most *un*biblical western misunderstanding of God's power and our *un*scriptural limitation of his creativity to a six-day period some millennia ago.

What did God intend by the opening sentences of Genesis? He intended exactly what the human author said: everything — dry land, plant and animal life, man himself — was created out of something already existing, even as his creativity continues to operate today. There was, and is, at least a "seed" already in existence.

Of the reader who yet clings to *ex nihilo* creation, the question is now asked, What will you have lost by releasing this traditional tenet? You have not lost the belief in biblical inerrancy, if indeed you have held this view. You have not lost your faith in the one holy and all-powerful God. You have not lost anything of lasting spiritual value. He is still to be worshiped as Earth's Almighty Creator. You have merely changed your mind — because of the overwhelming evidence — about a questionable point of doctrine. You have lost nothing more.

---

4 Stuhlmueller, *op. cit.*, p. 451.

5 Boman, *op. cit.* p. 173.

3. WHAT IS GENESIS' RELATIONSHIP TO PAGAN COSMOGONIES?

We have already noted most of the Old Testament's *poetic* references to creation. They reflect many similarities to neighboring pagan cosmogonies which have been uncovered by archaeologists since the mid-19th century. In addition to the Genesis narratives, Rahab-Leviathan-the serpent suggest a common pool of traditions throughout the ancient Middle East.[1] Heidel insists that one cannot fully understand Hebrew history without studying the literature of the nations surrounding Israel.[2] Briefly, the Babylonian creation epic abounds in apparent parallels to Gen. 1, as well as other Old Testament passages. For a century after this mythological cosmogony was first discovered, liberal Bible scholars were pointing out the "obvious" dependence of Genesis upon its Babylonian "ancestor."

In recent years however scholars have, with more wisdom, noted the impressive *differences* between the two. Dahood observes also that the Hebrew *tehom* is equivalent to *thm* of Ugaritic, an early northwest Semitic dialect quite similar to Hebrew. *Tehom* therefore "does not derive directly from Babylonian sources, as urged by generations of scholars."[3] Heidel too is satisfied that earlier scholars were wrong.[4] Sarna says it well: "The [biblical] Creation account is non-mythological... The outstanding peculiarity of the biblical account is the complete absence of mythology

---

[1] Cf. Umberto Cassuto, *op. cit.*, pp. 8f.

[2] Alexander Heidel, *op. cit.*, p. v.

[3] Dahood, *Psalms III*, Anchor Bible, *op. cit.*, p. 36. Cf. Fishbane, *op. cit.*, p. 159.

[4] Heidel, *op. cit.*, pp. 82f.

in the classical pagan sense of the term."[5]

Although Gen. 1 is strictly prose, a word should be added about Old Testament poetry, which includes nearly half of the Old Testament and almost all of the remaining Old Testament references to creation. Biblical poetry too has a quality quite different from what we moderns would expect. We think of modern poetry as being quite subjective, and it is. But the poetry of the Old Testament, particularly as found in the Prophets, is far more objective than that of our contemporaries. Job, Psalms and the Prophets reflect distinctive poetic styles intended to communicate rather clearly to their contemporaries. Biblical poetry is non-mythological, in spite of two centuries of liberal pronouncements to the contrary. For example, to speak of the "poetic" structure of Joshua 10, where it refers to "the long day," proves nothing. Poetry or prose, Joshua 10 speaks of an actual, natural event which armchair scientists have futilely tried to demythologize for generations.

The biblical references to creation actually picture, in the idiom of their time, the original, God-revealed primeval history of Earth. How then do we explain their similarities to the widespread Semitic and Mesopotamian creation myths?

Young responds to the question correctly: "The so-called cosmogonies of the various peoples of antiquity are in reality deformations of the originally revealed truth of creation."[6] Pagan religion always leads to mythological thinking.[7] Somewhere in great antiquity Man, apart from the true God, began to confuse Creator with creation, forming a

---

[5] Sarna, *op. cit.*, p. 9. Cf. Stigers, *op. cit.*, p. 48.

[6] E. J. Young, *op. cit.*, p. 82, note.

[7] The modern pagan religion known as secular humanism, for example, is replete with half-truths, or precisely what a future generation might call "myths."

mythological synthesis. Similar to the Bible these myths may be, yet the differences are vital. Pagan cosmogonies are ultimately dependent upon Earth's actual natural history, correctly recorded in Genesis.

Nearly a century ago the University of Chicago's Ira M. Price suggested the proper relationship between Genesis' creation narratives and the many other similar ancient creation myths.

> Their common elements seem to point to a time when the human race occupied a common home and held a common faith,...each handing on from age to age records concerning the early history of the race... One ancient religion did not borrow these universal traditions from another, but each possessed primitively these traditions in their original form. The Genesis record is the purest, the least colored by extravagances, and the nearest to what we must conceive to have been the original form of these accounts.[8]

Unger adds,

> The Genesis account is not only the purest, but everywhere bears the unmistakable impress of divine inspiration when compared with the extravagances and corruptions of other accounts. The Biblical narrative, we may conclude, represents the original form these traditions must have assumed.[9]

Even liberal scholars are impressed with the striking independence of the biblical narratives. Commenting on the Canaanite, Egyptian and Mesopotamian influences, Tucker adds with astonishment,

> But in view of Israel's location near the crossroads of the civilizations of the ancient world and her relatively weak political and cultural position, it is surprising

---

[8] Ira M. Price, Ovid R. Sellers, E. Leslie Carson, *The Monuments and the Old Testament*, Philadelphia: The Judson Press, 1958 (first published in 1899, revised in 1925 and 1958), p. 127.

[9] Merrill F. Unger, *Archaeology and the Old Testament*, Grand Rapids: Zondervan, 1954, p. 37. Cf. Heidel, *op. cit.*, pp. 71-118.

that the influence was not even more significant![10] Modern studies have solidly underscored the truth that Israel's unique faith and scriptures were not "religion," but developed rather as the result of direct intervention and revelation by God.

The fact that pagan cosmogonies appear to have some relationship to the correct description of the Creation should not offend our piety. Satan consistently displays the counterfeit, the half-truth. Nor should our piety be offended by the Old Testament allusions to pre-existent matter. The first chapter of Genesis varies from pagan cosmogonies in many respects, but creation out of nothing is *not* one of them.

Does this mean that matter is eternal, as ancient religions depict it? Or even as some contemporary atheistic evolution-ists would have it? Not at all! Marcus Dods says of Gen. 1, "The writer merely desires to refer the origin of the known world, *the heaven and the earth*, to God; and he does not consider the question of the eternity of matter."[11]

Pagan cosmogonies perceive Creator and creation as virtually identical: The Roman Pliny (1st century A.D.) says, "The world...is sacred, eternal... It is the work of nature, and itself constitutes nature."[12] But matter, according to the Bible, is not an absolute; it is distinct from and subservient to God.[13]

---

[10] Tucker, *op. cit.*, p. 22.

[11] Marcus Dods, *The Book of Genesis*, Edinburgh: T. & T. Clark, 1911, p. 1.

[12] *The Natural History of Pliny*, trans. John Bostock & H. T. Riley, London: George Bell & Sons, 1893, pp. 13-15.

[13] John Calvin, quoted in Eugene M. Klaaren, *Religious Origins of Modern Science*, Grand Rapids: Eerdmans, 1977, p. 43, gives a devastating critique of paganism's confusion of Creator and creation: "As if the universe, which was founded as a spectacle of God's glory, were its own creator!"

Scripture, as we have seen, makes no mention of a *past* eternity of matter, although Revelation seems to depict the *future* eternity of matter.

The ancient Greeks pondered much about such concepts. But speculation of this type is foreign to scripture.

> The Old Testament Jews were probably among the least speculative people known to history. The concrete earthiness with which they speak of sacred things can sometimes shock us. But there is a wisdom in [the opening words of Genesis] for which other races of men sought in vain.[14]

The great antiquity of matter proposed in this treatise may resemble pagan cosmogonies, but a denial of such antiquity because of such similarity is merely a reflection of a 19th century piety. Heaven may prove this denial to be correct, but it is not based upon even so much as one scriptural statement. It is simply pious speculation.

---

[14] Bruce Vawter, *A Path Through Genesis*, London: Sheed & Ward, 1957, p. 37. However, Jewish scholarship following the dispersion of A.D. 70 began to take on highly speculative qualities as reflected in the Mishnah and the Talmud.

4. IS THIS DUALISM?

It is almost a Sunday School cliche that the Bible is not dualistic.[1] We are told that the Babylonian Genesis is dualistic, with the "good" Marduk vanquishing the "evil" Tiamat and using her body as the raw material for creation. Zoroastrianism may be dualistic; Taoism too may be dualistic; but not the Bible. So we are told.

This is not true. The presence and power of personal evil are so obvious in scripture that one could wonder how such erroneous teaching developed. Certainly the Bible is dualistic! Spiritual warfare swirls about us.[2] The warfare transcends Earth's history. Creation was enveloped in warfare. The struggle continues to this day, and will culminate in the ultimate victory of Good and Earth's final, once-for-all re-creation.

Finegan says, "Dualism usually makes the creation evil..."[3] Not so! Finegan is referring to some of the *gnostic* systems which considered spirit good and matter evil. Platonic philosophy and Iranian religion encouraged such a dichotomy. But Martin Luther, in his call to the Church to return to biblical Christianity, bitterly attacked this horizontal division: he made the division vertical, and rightly so. Biblical dualism faces the fact that some *spiritual* entities are good and some are evil; some *physical* entities are good and others evil. Johannine theology provides excellent New Testament confirmation of Old Testament spiritual warfare.

---

[1] E.g., Hastings, *op. cit.*, p. 6.

[2] For an impressive exposition of biblical dualism see Donald Grey Barnhouse, *The Invisible War*, Grand Rapids: Zondervan, 1965. An entire volume is devoted to the subject.

[3] Jack Finegan, *In the Beginning*, N.Y.: Harper & Bros., 1962, p. 15.

Biblical dualism describes a good God seizing chaotic matter that had been under control of an evil spiritual power and forming it forcibly into something wholesome. The Bible further insists on another distinctly dualistic conception: that which is material can never become spiritual (1 Cor. 15:50).

Scientists today almost by definition live with a non-spiritual world view. A great leap of faith is usually required for a scientist — even one who is a creationist — to recognize the dominance of spiritual forces in this created universe. "The whole world is in the power of the evil one" (1 John 5:19), indeed, the entire biblical world view, can hardly be harmonized with the day-to-day scientific approach. A scientist who happens to be a Christian normally functions as if the physical were autonomous, his Sunday pronounce-ments notwithstanding. Admitting a loving, spiritual Creator is sometimes difficult for scientists trained in rationalistic philosophies; but accepting the dualistic activity of evil spiritual forces during the process of creation is perhaps more than most scientific creationists can receive, in spite of the biblical testimony.

Dualistic pagan religions make their gods "anthro-pomorphic." The whole pantheon engages in sexual activity, warfare, love, hate, jealousy, ambition, etc. Biblical commentators tend to be repelled by anthropomorphic behavior among the Old Testament "host of heaven," so they often attempt to allegorize, demythologize or simply ignore such references. Yet the Bible speaks clearly of those "angels that did not keep their own position" (Jude 6), but "took to wife such of them as they chose" (Gen. 6:2), producing giants in the earth (Gen. 6:4). Almighty God walks (Gen. 3:8), talks (1 Kings 22:20), has arms (Job 40:9), nostrils (Psalms 18:15), and feelings (Exodus 20:5; Lev. 26:30), loves (Hosea 11) and hates (Prov. 6:16), and yes, even conducts warfare (Judges 4:15; Isaiah 42:13; Rev. 12:7). God acted still more anthropomorphically and created man in his own image, which means that "the man looks like God" (Gen. 1:27).[4]

Gnostic studies define dualism as spiritual vs. material, considering that which is spiritual as "good" and that which is physical, material as "evil." But the God of the Bible cares deeply about the material: He is now in the process of redeeming the physical earth.

Many of us Christians — too much like the ancient gnostics — perceive a God who is too distant, too impotent, too uninvolved.[5] Yet the God of the Bible condescended to create a world He could become involved in, and a man enough like Himself that God could perceive Himself in a father role. Against the charge of "anthropomorphism!" we could assert that the greatest anthropomorphism of all is that God became Man in Jesus of Nazareth!

Almighty God even became *weary* during Creation Week, in spite of some attempts to generalize from Isaiah 40:28. Nearly all modern commentators tell how the LORD God created "effortlessly," speaking only the word, and it was accomplished.[6] Again, the biblical evidence suggests otherwise. Effortless creation is another modern myth.[7]

Prior to the 18th century Enlightenment writers, artists and sculptors portrayed God on the seventh day of creation as *tired*. Medieval and Renaissance sculpture has been described by White.

---

[4] Cf. G. Ch. Aalders, *op. cit.*, p. 71.

[5] See e.g., J. B. Phillips, *Your God Is Too Small*, N.Y.: Macmillan, 1953.

[6] E.g., Skinner, *op. cit.*, p. 15; S. R. Driver, *The Book of Genesis*, London: Methuen, 1904, p. 5, note; Dillman, *op. cit.*, p. 60; Spurrell, *op. cit.*, p. 3; Ridderbos, *op. cit.*, p. 30.

[7] Cardona, *op. cit.*, *Kronos*, Vol. IV, p. 74.

> The furrows of thought on the Creator's brow show
> that in this work he is obliged to contrive; the knotted
> muscles upon his arms show that he is obliged to toil;
> naturally, then, the sculptors and painters of the
> mediaeval and early modern period frequently repre-
> sented him as the writers whose conceptions they
> embodied had done — as, on the seventh day, weary
> after thought and toil, enjoying well-earned repose
> and the plaudits of the hosts of heaven.[8]

> The Almighty...is shown as seated in almost the exact
> attitude of the "Weary Mercury" of classic sculpture
> — bent, and with a very marked expression of fatigue
> upon his countenance and in the whole disposition of
> his body.[9]

Again, effortless creation is a *modern* myth. The Spirit's
exertion must have been great as He moved across the face of
the waters. The physical violence as the dry land was being
lifted would have been incredibly spectacular. The stubborn-
ness of the waters was not easy to overcome. The four (or
five) chaotic entities noted in Gen. 1:2 imply a mighty
resistance to God's efforts.

Our Creator was quite serious when, as scripture says,
He rested on the seventh day. Yet many modern scholars
treat that first sabbath as a mere literary device for man's
instruction.[10] This is ironic in view of the fact that
conservative writers usually interpret the remainder of the
creation narrative quite literally. Although Gen. 1 does not
mention specific effort or struggle by the Spirit of God, one
cannot argue from silence that the acts of creation were
accomplished without exertion.

The biblical keys to understanding God's personal

---

[8] White, *op. cit.*, Vol. I, p. 1.

[9] *Ibid.*, p. 3, note.

[10] Cf. e.g., Arthur S. Peake, *A Commentary on the Bible*, London:
T. C. & E. C. Jack, 1931, p. 135.

sabbath are found, first, in Gen. 2:2: "He rested on the seventh day from all his work which he had done"; second, in the poetic references to creation, replete with allusions to violence, noted in Chapter IX; third, the clear statement of Exodus 20:11, where it is said that "...in six days the LORD made heaven and earth, the sea, and all that is in them, and rested the seventh day; therefore the LORD blessed the sabbath day and hallowed it"; and fourth, note God's own words in Exodus 31:17: "It is a sign for ever between me and the people of Israel that in six days the LORD made heaven and earth, and on the seventh day he rested, *and was refreshed."*

The Bible is to be interpreted quite literally unless otherwise implied by the context!

Still there is more. A working Father is complemented by a working Son.

> Jesus said to them, "My food is to do the will of him who sent me, and to accomplish his work... My Father is working still, and I am working... We must work the works of him who sent me, while it is yet day; night comes when no one can work" (John 4:34; 5:17; 9:4).

The Holy Spirit, the third Person of the Trinity, is the "executive arm" of the Godhead, and the One whose workings are most visible to man.

Further, a working man was created to represent and rule on behalf of and in the power of the working God.

> And God blessed them, and God said to them, "Be fruitful and multiply, and fill the earth and subdue it; and have dominion over the fish of the sea and over the birds of the air and over every living thing that moves upon the earth" (Gen. 1:28).

> For we are his workmanship, created in Christ Jesus for good works, which God prepared beforehand, that we should walk in them (Eph. 2:10).

> Therefore, my beloved, as you have always obeyed, so now...work out your own salvation with fear and

trembling; for God is at work in you, both to will and to work for his good pleasure (Phil. 2:12,13).

The point is that God is more actively involved in this universe, in this earth, in this human race, than our rationalistic minds can appreciate. He was involved in the struggle of creation, is still involved in his continuing work as Sustainer, as well as the culminating battles that are even now shaking the earth and the heavens. The presence of powerful evil, the horrible death of his own Son, the present condition of the human race, all indicate that God is prepared to suffer losses in order to win the war. He grieves every moment He loses a soul who has chosen death rather than life. Portions of Job, Psalms and Isaiah fairly reek with allusions to violent spiritual warfare; and, of course, the New Testament portrays great violence in both spiritual and material realms. The charge of anthropomorphism is meaningless. The immanent God is powerfully involved in his creation!

It is hoped that this entire presentation is enabling the reader to perceive the great sweep of Earth's violent history from Creation to Culmination — the majesty, the purpose-fulness, the agony, the pathos, and the victory of its loving, persevering Creator. Biblical dualism is highly visible from beginning to end.

5. IS THERE A CONFLICT BETWEEN THEOLOGY AND GEOLOGY?

It has often been proclaimed during the past two centuries that science and religion do not belong together. Gunkel states the case.

> The conflict between theology and geology is eliminated when both stay within their boundaries. Religion has to leave it to science to speak about the creation of the world and man as best as it can. But natural science, if it observes its boundaries, should neither affirm nor deny the dogma about creation.[1]

Gunkel is in error. Science and religion have *always* been synthesized in human culture, as is still the case.

Galileo is a good case in point. Modern worshipers at the altar of "Science" would have us believe that Galileo tried to demonstrate the astronomical fact that the Solar System is heliocentric, and that the Roman Inquisition opposed the march of scientific truth. This accusation against the Roman Catholic Church is far removed from reality. Yet such we have all learned from our science textbooks.

Actually, Galileo's 17th century confirmation of heliocentricity by the use of his telescope was at first welcomed by the Church at Rome, in particular the Jesuit astronomers. However, the scientific faculty at the University of Bologna was severely critical of this sarcastic rebel. The disagreement over heliocentricity was between a scientist and the scientific community. Finally, in order to bring the explosive issue to a resolution, Pope Urban VIII asked for a position paper from the science faculty at the University. The paper was totally geocentric and filled with distortions, appealing to "scientific"

---

[1] Hermann Gunkel, *Genesis*, Göttingen: Vanderhoeck & Ruprecht, 6th ed., 1964, p. 131 (trans. from the German). Cf. also Von Rad, *op. cit.*; Hyers, *op. cit.*; *et al.*

tradition, to Aristotle and, interestingly, to religious tradition.[2]

> Urban VIII and his court may be considered much less the oppressors of science than the first bewildered casualties of the scientific age... The original challenge went far back in time. [Galileo] had become a danger when he started writing in Italian [rather than Latin, the language of science] and when he decided to bypass the universities and vested intellectual authority and reveal his mind to enlightened public opinion.[3]

> It has been known for a long time that a major part of the Church intellectuals were on the side of Galileo, while the clearest opposition to him came from secular ideas.[4]

Galileo was condemned by the Inquisition not so much for teaching error as for reneging on an earlier pledge not to speak so brashly and publicly of his revolutionary insights. "He realized at last that the authorities were not interested in truth but only in authority."[5]   Churchmen of many persuasions spoke bitterly of Galileo later, but not until the science faculty at the University and the Jesuit astronomers had falsely made his case *religious*, and the ecclesiastics were provoked into perceiving that his teachings might be threatening the authority of the Roman Church.   17th century scientists thoroughly enjoyed their ability to generate such civil and ecclesiastical recriminations, as some in the university communities still do to this day. Galileo's tragedy is not one of Church vs. Science, but rather the religious

---

[2] Jerry Bergman, "The Establishment of a Heliocentric View of the Universe," *Journal of the American Scientific Affiliation*, Vol. 33, No. 4, pp. 225-30.

[3] Giorgio de Santillana, *The Crime of Galileo*, Chicago: Univ. of Chicago Press, 1955, p. 204.

[4] *Ibid.*, p. xii.

[5] *Ibid.*, p. 257.

traditionalism of scientists who typically resent revolutionary ideas.⁶ His experience has a distinctly modern ring to it.

The 17th century, in retrospect, almost opened the floodgates for creationism. Western man was slowly learning the historical and scientific methods. Honest historians of science have long recognized that these important advances were due almost exclusively to scholars immersed in Reformed theology or the Pietistic Revival of the late 17th century. In spite of the devastation of Europe's Thirty Years' War, this became the century of the giants of Christian historical and scientific scholarship. Descartes, Kepler, Galileo, Leibnitz, Newton, Burnet, Whiston, Arnold, and countless other scientist-philosophers who *took the Bible seriously* were slowly learning how to discover God's truths in the heavens above and the earth beneath. Building upon one another's researches and philosophizings, these devout pioneers seemed headed in the right direction.

However, the traditional concept of a "tranquil" Flood was standing in the path of scientific understanding of Earth's early history. A careful exegesis of Gen. 7:11,19,20; 8:3,5; and Matt. 24:39a would have provided a guide to the violent *tidal* nature of the Flood. Gen. 8:5a says, quite literally, "And the waters were going and diminishing until the tenth month..." Jesus made a pertinent statement, recorded in Matt. 24:39a: "[A]nd they did not know until the flood came and swept them all away..." An awareness of these seven-and-a-half months of enormous (and probably intermittent) tidal action in turn would have led 17th century scholars to the correct perception of the stratigraphy of Earth's huge sedimentary deposits.

They also were ignorant of the other ancient Jewish records that told of the *igneous* eruptions accompanying the Flood. Assuming that the Deluge was due exclusively to a

---

⁶ Bergman, *op. cit.*, pp. 225f.

tranquil rainfall rather than the more destructive "fountains of the great deep" bursting forth, the varied strata, with fossils they contained, bewildered 17th century scientists (and nearly all since) concerning the cause of their deposition and the resultant true age of life on the earth.[7]

Still, sooner or later their Christian descendants should have produced a viable creation model, one that would fit both biblical and the growing natural evidence. William Buckland, an early 19th century clergyman-geologist, accurately perceived — as a direct result of Earth's empirical evidence — the catastrophic nature of the Deluge; but he apparently overlooked the important scriptural details of Gen. 7 and 8. To this day students of the philosophy of science still miss the truth:

> It required another scholarly clergyman, the Revd John Fleming,...to call into question the closeness of correspondence between the Mosaic testimony and the geological and paleontological evidence. Moses left word of a gentle strand of water rising placidly for 40 days, with the flood leaving no trace except a rainbow. This was hardly the account of a violent and transient storm.[8]

The Christians who studied geology could not answer this objection effectively, leading even Buckland into forsaking flood geology.[9] Such a common misinterpretation of the Genesis Flood has ruled to this day. Careful biblical exegesis and rabbinical studies would have indicated that the global fires and seven-and-a-half months of violent tidal action must have caused incalculably more damage than 40

---

[7] The Old Testament writers were quite aware that the greater danger to the earth during the Deluge came, not from the skies, but from the seas. See e.g., Job 7:12; 26:12; 38:8-11; Psalms 68:22; 104:6-9; Prov. 8:29; Isaiah 27:1; Jer. 5:22.

[8] Hallam, *op. cit.*, p. 43.

[9] *Ibid.*, p. 51.

days of rainfall alone. Buckland's biblical beliefs were thus increasingly perceived as a handicap to understanding. Witnessing a growing rationalistic antisupernaturalism, the 18th and early 19th centuries began closing the door on creationism. The scientific study of origins was thereby dealt a crippling and nearly-permanent blow by antisupernaturalism's stifling apriorism.

Rationalism's restrictive rules led inexorably to the twin 19th century philosophies of uniformitarianism and evolution, the latter a regression back to ancient religious beliefs. Those two pagan concepts, now dressed in modern clothing, are both quite religious; they are contemporary religious dogma, statements of faith. Uniformitarianism and evolution are built only upon highly selective data; they are little more than modern mythological constructions, guided by and themselves expressing the underlying religious beliefs and desires of their worshipers. Uniformitarianism and evolution are the contemporary humanist's perception of reality, containing modern distortions of truth much as we find distortions in ancient pagan cosmologies around the world.

The modern religion of secular humanism resembles its ancient pagan precursors in that all are evolutionary. In fact, only the Judaeo-Christian biblical tradition is *non*-evolutionary, even as Judge William R. Overton correctly noted in his infamous decision in the 1982 Arkansas Creation Science trial. All religion is evolutionary. Man, left to his own devices, can never discover who he is, where he came from, or where he is going. He will always reason his way into an evolutionary trap. Though his denials may be loud, yet the reality remains that the humanist's evolutionary world view is his religion — and is thus holy, untouchable.

Today a scientist may safely challenge any dogma except the two that are sacred, uniformitarianism and evolution. If a scientist, writing alone, dares to confront either of those doctrines, he may expect the full pressure of the modern Inquisition.   Secular catastrophists as well as creationists have in this generation been calling attention to contradictory data, although their contributions remain largely scorned or unacknowledged. Because of the sheer weight of evidence — catastrophic burials, mass extinctions of life, etc. — uniformitarianism in the sense Hutton, Lyell and Darwin wrote of it has in recent years come under moderate attack, particularly by Goldschmidt's "hopeful monster" theory and its up-to-date stepchild, Gould's "punctuated equilibrium." But these incredible *ad hoc* hypotheses would constitute mere hiccups in the vast uniformitarian time scheme; the basic half-billion-year-plus geologic time column remains sacrosanct to this day.

While many scientists speak scornfully about such a possibility, yet Immanuel Velikovsky *et al.* have written persuasively on the subject of historical catastrophism, adducing extensive biblical, mythological, historical and geological evidence.   Writing *prior to* the Space Age, Velikovsky compiled a truly-remarkable (even if not recognized) record of many dozens of explicit and implicit predictions about the nature of the Solar System.[10]   While Velikovsky's reconstructions of Earth's recent history may be riddled with errors, and his "catastrophic evolution" may merely resemble Goldschmidt's and Gould's theories, still his *confirmed prior descriptions* of the Solar System can be denied only by those who are wilfully blind. See especially his *World s in Collision* and *Earth in Upheaval*;[11] for a similar although creationist position see Donald W. Patten; all in Bibliography.

---

[10] Cf., e.g., Thomas Ferté, "A Record of Success," *Pensée*, Special Issue, Vol. II, No. 2, May 1972, pp. 11-15, 23.

[11] Garden City, N.Y.: Doubleday & Co., 1950 and 1955.

Peer pressure among scientists provides a suffocating blanket of repression, effectively retarding the progress of science through the ages. A cursory study of the history of science — to this day — demonstrates this truth, which has been witnessed once again in our very generation on the subject of Alfred Wegener's theory of continental drift (plate tectonics). Hallam's *Great Geological Controversies* eloquently and in detail presents the furor concerning a theory now rather widely received, although by no means proven nor totally accepted in the world of science.[12]

> ...In the early 1950's continental drift was taken seriously by very few. The minute number of staunch adherents tended to be dismissed as cranks... A large number of people were either noncommital or had a sneaking sympathy with the ideas of Wegener and du Toit, but considered it professionally wise to keep fairly quiet about it. (p. 148)...One of Wegener's strongest critics, R. T. Chamberlin,...quoted with evident approval an overheard remark...in 1926. "If we are to believe Wegener's hypothesis we must forget everything which has been learned in the last seventy years and start all over again." (p. 151)... The American paleontologist G. G. Simpson noted in 1943 the near unanimity of paleontologists against Wegener's ideas... "The known past and present distribution of land mammals cannot be explained by the hypothesis of drifting continents." Bailey Willis was even more outspoken than Simpson. "...My reason refuses to consider 'continental drift' possible... The geology upon which protagonists of the theory rest assumptions is as antiquated as pre-Curie physics... Thus the theory of continental drift is a fairy tale..." (pp. 135-6).
>
> In nearly all matters the human mind has a strong tendency to judge in the light of its own experience, knowledge and prejudices rather than on the evidence

---

[12] Anthony Hallam, *Great Geological Controversies*, Oxford and New York: Oxford Univ. Press, 1983, pp. 110f.

presented. Thus new ideas are judged in the light of prevailing beliefs. If the ideas are too revolutionary, that is to say, if they depart too far from reigning theories and cannot be fitted into the current body of knowledge, they will not be acceptable. When discoveries are made before their time they are almost certain to be ignored or meet with opposition which is too strong to overcome, so in most instances they might as well not have been made. (p. 152, quoted from Beveridge, *The Art of Scientific Investigation*).[13]

Alfred Wegener was neither geologist nor paleontologist. His formal training was in astronomy and meteorology, perhaps explaining why the present work had to be written by a non-specialist.

The knowledge explosion of our generation has been most kind to the creationist viewpont. It is sparking a revolution that deeply offends the religiosity of many evolutionary scientists. Evolutionists thus seem less anxious to respond to creationists with the facts than they are exercised by the "religious" effort of trying to stamp out creationism. Their attacks are largely *ad hominem*, or they set up straw men to demolish, both of which are prominent characteristics of religious bigotry.

The biblical faith is unique. It is *not* religion. In fact, religion is perceived as a major problem throughout the narrative portions of the Bible. "Religion" is normally man's attempt to find a god (or gods) and to discover how to control it (or them). In the scriptures we observe precisely the opposite. We perceive the one true God who cannot be found by man (Isaiah 45:15a; 55:8,9), and thus cannot be controlled, but rather who has chosen to reveal Himself to man (1 Cor. 1:21). He is the Creator, a highly moral Personality, concerned about the truth, for He Himself is Truth (Isaiah 65:16a; John 14:6,17).

---

[13] W. I. B. Beveridge, *The Art of Scientific Investigation*, London: Heinemann, 1950, p. 152.

Thus we may accept the scientific data God gives us in his personal self-revelation, the Bible. The information about our natural world found in scripture is never described explicitly as such, but usually is presented in an offhand, incidental manner. Nor is the Bible self-consciously a textbook or even a volume of theology, but rather is largely a telling of the mighty acts of God, from which we may glean surprisingly accurate historical, theological, scientific and other data.

> Man can study this information and upon the basis of his study can make true statements concerning Creation. The study of this revealed material is as truly the study of history as is the study of Caesar's accounts of ancient Gaul.[14]

Therefore, since science and religion (not the biblical revelation) are historically found commingled, their joint conclusions cannot always be trusted, and consequently must be re-examined continually. But science and the Bible together allow much more accurate conclusions, and a most viable model of Earth's origins can be extrapolated from sincere Bible study and historical research in conjunction with all, not selective, available data from the natural world. We cannot legitimately separate theology from geology: the Spiritual created the Physical.

Nor can theology — or geology, for that matter — be separated from the *miraculous*, particularly when the biblical evidence points clearly to an obviously miraculous paleo-geologic event. Now we touch the heart of another problem. Most evolutionists *assume* — with the deists — that God's supernatural intervention never occurred; most creationists *assume* — with the dispensationalists — that He used to intervene but does so no longer. These two *a prioris* are both unwarranted, as demonstrated by biblical, paleontological

---

[14] E. J. Young, *op. cit.*, p. 24.

and contemporary evidence. They are crippling our research concerning origins, and crippling the modern Church as well.

The burden of bankrupt 18th century assumptions lies heavily upon modern science. A scientist — be he evolutionist or creationist — who rejects contemporary miracles out-of-hand has already prejudiced his conclusions, severely restricting the possibility of his arriving at correct results in his investigation of Earth's origins. Current manifestations of the Lord's miraculous power provide us with helpful suggestions for our study. God was, and continues to be, sovereign!

To restate the whole problem of the age of the earth and its solution, we need to examine critically all of our axioms. Since the Bible is truth and it obviously tells of a young earth, and since some scientific data have accumulated indicating an old earth, we must check out every aprioristic statement. The resolution must never be a strained *ad hoc* compromise, but rather must be sought in the simplest, most evidential answers. Occam's razor still shaves painfully close. The truth may be disconcerting, even iconoclastic, and probably will injure a sacred cow-or-two; but, after all, truth is what we want.

6. WHICH EARTH?

When we deal with the question of the age of the earth, the inquiry is painfully enlarged by asking a further question: Which earth?

This may sound like a foolish question, but to any of the ancients it would have been all-important. The peoples of antiquity around the globe thought in terms of a *cycle* of world destructions and re-creations. We have already noted Origen's cyclical view, which of course tended to conform to already-ancient Greek and Egyptian traditions. 2 Peter 3:3-13 provides possible hints of three "earths" or "worlds." Catastrophists point to several biblical stories which, although localized in their viewpoints, might well have been describing worldwide cataclysms. Patten *et al.* suggest a number of catastrophes in addition to the Flood, among which are included the tower of Babel, Sodom-Gomorrah, the Exodus and the long day of Joshua.[1] If indeed these events were global in scope, the ancients would have considered every one to be the end of one "earth" or "earth-age" and the beginning of another.

There are innumerable allusions to these catastrophes in very ancient literature worldwide. And our planet does bear enormous scars that speak eloquently of such violent upheavals. Uniformitarianism in Earth's natural history has apparently, however, been the rule since Isaiah's time; neither the Bible nor any other human history records a subsequent catastrophe of global proportions. There have been no further "new earths." Scripture of course promises the one more — and final — cosmic destruction and "new earth" to come.

The *pre-flood* earth — what the ancients called the

---

[1] Patten, Hatch & Steinhauer, *The Long Day of Joshua and Six Other Catastrophes*, Seattle: Pacific Meridian. 1973

"Golden Age" — was uniformly warmer and much more hospitable, as both Bible and paleontology amply confirm.[2] The earth *as we know it* is primarily the post-Flood re-creation, geologically quite recent, with lesser subsequent convulsions such as the division of continents (Gen. 10:25), well-attested by modern geology, the strange natural events during Joshua's generation, and the 8th century B.C. upheavals described in Amos 1:1; Zech. 14:5; and Isaiah 24.

Because of its violent natural history, guided by the hand of God, Earth's age is confused, and quite difficult to ascertain. Some measurements of age would be valid only as far into the past as the most recent global catastrophe. Additional geological yardsticks would have been affected by ancient mountain range deformations and the Flood, with its massive volcanic upheavals. Still further into the past the creation catastrophe would provide the *terminus a quo* for certain determinations. Other measurements, such as stellar distances, computed in multi-millions of light years, would be utterly unaffected by cosmic "accidents" occurring within the relatively small confines of our Solar System.[3] Thus old earth and young earth proponents can both hurl valid age measurements at each other, leading to an unresolved conflict, with apparently solid evidences appearing on each side of the controversy. Our catastrophic history simply has had varying effects on Earth's measurements of age.

Earlier there was mentioned the marginal concern about radiometric dating, in particular the uranium-lead, potassium-argon and rubidium-strontium dating techniques. Although

---

[2] Whitcomb & Morris, *op. cit.*, present the biblical and paleontological evidences for the warmth of the Adam-to-Noah age, pp. 239f.

[3] Patten, *The Biblical Flood and The Ice Epoch*, Seattle: Pacific Meridian, 1966, suggests "galactogenesis," a cosmic calendar which conforms somewhat to the present findings. See pp. 295f.

some serious questions about these methods have already been noted, this work renders much of the creationist argument against radiometric dating as moot, because the Hebraic exegesis of Gen. 1:1-3 allows for such very old dates in Earth's stones, if not in its bones.

Uniformitarians traditionally have denied the recent global convulsions that are so obviously part of the geological record, although today increasing numbers are realizing how untenable is that position in the face of the earth's mute testimony. It is good to see a slow awakening to the truth, although catastrophic evidences are usually considered by evolutionists to be local, rarely if ever worldwide, or, if global, then very ancient geologically.

The point to be stressed is that the entire earth has repeatedly — including during the Creation — suffered enormous shocks. These catastrophic events have affected our time measurements variously. Perhaps those scientists who are interested in paleochronology will begin to ask the question any ancient would have asked: Which earth are we talking about? — the chaos before the Creation? — or, the comfortable world of Adam and his successors? — or, the badly scarred and severely degraded earth of Noah's descendants?

The question is troublesome. Which earth indeed?

XI THE WATERS

Gen. 1:2 speaks of "the deep," the typical translation of the Hebrew *tehom*. Driver says that *tehom* as used here does not mean what the deep or the sea would denote to the modern world, but rather "...the primitive *undivided* waters, the huge watery mass which the writer conceived as enveloping the earth."[1] Driver of course perceives these waters mythologically, so we must demythologize *his* language. In modern terms, we find that prior to Gen. 1:6,7 these waters covered the earth, forming a hydrosphere upon this planet *and* a hot, steamy atmosphere above "the face of the waters" — an utterly uninhabitable chaos.

Following the creation of light, God dealt firmly with *tehom*, those chaotic waters. Two acts were necessary to make the earth habitable: the separation of the vaporous waters above the earth from the waters below, and the raising of the land and the forcing of the oceans into their allotted areas. In verse 7 "God made the sky [firmament]," and He used the sky to "separate [i.e., establish order between] the waters *under* the sky from the waters *above* the sky." The waters above were called *mabbul*, a specific Hebrew designation to distinguish them from the remaining waters of *tehom* below, the oceans. The words of verse 7 describe the establishment of the antediluvian "vapor canopy,"[2] first

---

[1] Driver, *op. cit.*, p. 4.

[2] The vapor canopy is suggested by these scriptures in Genesis: 2:5,6,10; 3:8; 6:17; 7:6-12,17; 8:2; 9:11,15,28; 10:1,32; 11:10. Additional intimations are found in Psalms 18:11; 29:10 and 2 Peter 3:5,6. The picture becomes even clearer when read in a literal translation.

suggested in the modern era by Isaac Newton Vail more than
a century ago.[3] Water vapor is indeed somewhat lighter than
air. This canopy, *mabbul*, was condensed out during the
Deluge, but the flood chapters of Genesis correctly recall its
former existence. Dillow recently hypothesized a 40-foot
column of water vapor six miles above the earth in a
temperature inversion,[4] which separated *mabbul* from the
remainder of *tehom*, although some knowledgeable creationists
are disputing Dillow's calculations. Von Rad exegetes the
scripture brilliantly.

> An understanding...of the Flood depends materially
> on the correct translation of the word *mabbul*.
> *Mabbul* does not mean "flood," "inundation," or even
> "destruction," but it is a technical term for a part of
> the world structure, namely, the heavenly ocean. This
> heavenly sea, which is above the firmament (*raqia'*),
> empties downward... We must understand the Flood,
> therefore, as a catastrophe involving the entire
> cosmos. When the heavenly ocean breaks forth upon
> the earth below, and the primal sea beneath the earth,
> which is restrained by God, now freed from its bonds,
> gushes up through yawning chasms onto the earth,
> then there is a destruction of the entire cosmic
> system according to biblical cosmogony. The two
> halves of the chaotic primeval sea, separated — the one
> up, the other below — by God's creative government,
> are again united; creation begins to sink again into

[3] Isaac N. Vail, *The Earth's Annular System*, 4th ed., Pasadena: Annular World Co., 1912, p. v. Vail first wrote of the canopy in 1874. Jerome, the translator of the 4th century Latin Vulgate, proposed a canopy, *compactae et densiores aquae: Letters*, LXIX, 6, in J.-P. Migne, *Patrologia Latina*, Vol. XXII, p. 659, noted by White, *op. cit.*, Vol. I, p. 324. White infers Jerome's words to mean "ice." The philosopher Immanuel Kant suggested two centuries ago that the Flood might have been caused by the collapse of a vapor "ring," similar to Saturn's (Haber, *op. cit.*, p. 150). Vail was attracted to Kant's theory, although he had proposed it independently.

[4] Dillow, *op. cit.*, pp. 247f.

chaos. Here the catastrophe, therefore, concerns not only men and beasts..., but the earth — indeed, the entire cosmos.[5]

In other words, the Deluge is directly connected with Creation. It is, in fact, the exact reversal of it.[6]

Mabbul is found 13 times in the Old Testament. It is dealt with in detail because of its common mistranslation, noted by von Rad.

(1) For behold, I will bring *mabbul* of waters upon the earth... (Gen. 6:17a).

(2) Noah was six hundred years old when *mabbul* of waters came upon the earth (Gen. 7:6).

(3) And Noah...went into the ark, to escape the waters of *mabbul* (Gen. 7:7).

(4) And after seven days the waters of *mabbul* came upon the earth (Gen. 7:10).

(5) *Mabbul* continued forty days upon the earth (Gen. 7:17a).

(6) ...[N]ever again shall all flesh be cut off by the waters of *mabbul*,

(7) and [literally, there is no longer *mabbul* to wipe out] the earth (Gen. 9:11b,c).

(8) [Literally]...No longer shall there be the waters — namely *mabbul* [in apposition to the waters] — to wipe out all flesh (Gen. 9:15b).

(9) After *mabbul* Noah lived three hundred and fifty years (Gen. 9:28).

(10) ...[S]ons were born to them after *mabbul* (Gen. 10:1b).

(11) ...[A]nd from these the nations spread abroad on the earth after *mabbul* (Gen. 10:32b).

(12) ...[H]e became the father of Arpachshad two years after *mabbul* (Gen. 11:10c).

---

[5] Von Rad, *op. cit.*, p. 124. Cf. Delitzsch, *op. cit.*, p. 78.

[6] Sarna, *op. cit.*, p. 55.

> (13) The LORD sat enthroned over *mabbul*;
>   the LORD is enthroned as King forever
>   (Psalms 29:10 NIV, note).[7]

The New International Version's scholars translate Psalms
29:10a traditionally in the text, but insert their scholarship in
the footnote; even the LXX translators were ignorant of the
by-then ancient meaning of the word. 2 Peter 3:5-13, which is
such a helpful New Testament commentary on the Creation
and the Flood, confirms the two "waters" — *tehom* and
mabbul.

> ...[A]n earth formed out of water and by means
> of water, through which [Gk. *di hon*, plural] the
> world that then existed was deluged with water and
> perished" (2 Peter 3:5c,6).

The writer's choice of the genitive plural "which" again shows
his astute perception of the actual conditions prior to the
Flood.   He had not lost the national memory of the
antediluvian vapor canopy, even if the LXX translators had.[8]
Mabbul then is the specific term or title for "the waters
above," and our English versions should use the words "the
canopy" or an appropriate synonym each time *mabbul*
appears.

As may be seen from Gen. 9:11c and 9:15b, *mabbul* no
longer exists.   It was condensed out some millennia ago.

---

[7] Cf. Dahood, *Psalms I*, Anchor Bible, *op. cit.*, pp. 175, 180;
Craigie, *op. cit.*, pp. 242-49; Robert Young, *Young's Literal
Translation of the Holy Bible*, Revised Edition, Grand Rapids:
Baker, 1956, p. 362.   Brown, Driver and Briggs, *op. cit.*, translate
Psalms 29:10a, "The LORD at the Flood sat enthroned,"
considering that *mabbul* "seems in all other passages to be almost
equal to a proper name of the Flood" (p. 550).   Their statement,
while not revealing the whole picture, as does von Rad's, is still
quite helpful in understanding the nature of *mabbul*.   The definite
article is missing in 9:11c and 9:15b, suggesting a titular quality
for *mabbul*.

[8] Cf. James Moffatt, *The General Epistles,* The Moffatt New
Testament Commentary, N.Y.: Harper & Brothers, n.d., p. 204.

Today the atmosphere scarcely contains even inches of water vapor. Without a perception of the antediluvian canopy, however, Bible students are mystified about the significance of Creation's second day's work.

Von Rad has confirmed from his exegesis of Genesis that the Flood involved the entire cosmos. 2 Peter 3:5,6 likewise pictures the entire cosmos having been violently re-ordered during the Flood, and then verse 7 gives the most specific New Testament portrayal of the future destruction by fire *of the entire cosmos.*

The Creation-Flood sequence may contribute toward the resolution of another disagreement regarding translation in Gen. 1. Many liberal scholars translate *ruach Elohim* of Gen. 1:2 as "the wind of God," while traditionalists read "the Spirit of God." (See Appendix). By itself *ruach* may legitimately be translated either way, the context dictating the choice throughout the Old Testament. Commentators often justify their preferences in verse 2, but without convincing proof.

Meaningful hints of the correct translation of *ruach* may be found once again by following the same two lines of investigation: first, studying the larger biblical context and, second, utilizing the modern sciences of paleontology and meteorology. Gen. 1-9 provides several suggestions that rain may not have existed before the Deluge — in particular the newly-displayed rainbow. Noah probably would have had no comprehension of the impending rainfall God was describing in Gen. 7:4 had the Lord not used the technical term *mabbul* in Gen. 6:17 when explaining what He was about to do. Rain — certainly *heavy* rain — would have been foreign to Noah's 600 years of experience.

Paleontology demonstrates that the entire antediluvian earth was rather uniformly warm or temperate. Remains of the woolly mammoth, a large animal requiring a temperate climate, are found by the tens of thousands north of the 70th parallel. Extensive coal deposits, containing tropical and subtropical vegetation, are among the surprises of frigid Antarctica. Rain is carried by and is a result of wind, and wind is caused by temperature differentials. If the temperatures between the poles were fairly uniform, there would have been little or no breeze, and thus probably no rain.

All of this suggests that *ruach Elohim* should be translated, not "the wind of God" (since there may have been no wind), but rather the only remaining option, "the Spirit of God."[9]

The Creation-Deluge sequence in Gen. 1-9 actually reveals a pattern of chaos to cosmos to chaos to cosmos. As the flood waters rose and receded God was re-creating the earth with quite different topographical and climatic characteristics. Anderson observes that the Flood narrative "flows in a sequence of units toward a turning-point and then follows the same sequence in reverse."[10] Quoting McEvenue,[11] he calls this pattern chiastic, or "palindromic."

Transitional Introduction (6:9-10)
  1. Violence in God's creation (6:11-12)
    2. First divine address: resolution to destroy (6:13-22)
      3. Second divine address: command to enter the ark (7:1-10)
        4. Beginning of the flood (7:11-16)
          5. The rising flood waters (7:17-24)
             GOD'S REMEMBRANCE OF NOAH
          6. The receding flood waters (8:1-5)

---

[9] There may have been, *prior to* God's "leashing" on Day Three, strong winds (and tides) sweeping over the watery earth, but these chaotic gales should hardly be described as "the wind of God"; they are part of the chaos.

[10] Bernhard W. Anderson, "From Analysis to Synthesis: the Interpretation of Genesis 1-11," *Journal of Biblical Literature*, 97, 1978, p. 37.

[11] Sean E. McEvenue, "The Narrative Style of the Priestly Writer," *Analecta Biblica*, 50, 1971, pp. 27-32.

7. The drying of the earth (8:6-14)
8. Third divine address: command to leave the ark (8:15-19)
9. God's resolution to preserve order (8:20-22)
10. Fourth divine address: covenant blessing and peace (9:1-17)
Transitional Conclusion (9:18-19)

The first part of the story represents a movement toward chaos...
The second part represents a movement toward a new creation.[12]

Noah stepped out of the ark into a brand-new world, now more water than land after 40 days of rain. The sons of Noah, no longer threatened by hostile "giants," found a new threat — an increasingly severe climatic regime.

We are reminded by this flood sequence of von Rad's assessment of Gen. 1:2: "Thus this second verse speaks not only of a reality that once existed in a preprimeval period, but also of a possibility that always exists."[13] Zimmerli warns, "You who feel so secure under your heaven, do you know that God holds this whole world together? And that the space in which you breathe is totally in his hand and He does as He pleases?"[14] Although God has assured us in Gen. 9:11 that "there is no longer *mabbul* to wipe out the earth," and some day *tehom* will be no more (Rev. 21:1), yet there remains the *tohu wabohu* of Gen. 1:2 and the prospect of future judgment, not by water, but by fire.

---

[12] Anderson, *op. cit.*, pp. 37, 38; Gordon J. Wenham gives an alternative and more detailed structure: "The Coherence of the Flood Narrative," *Vetus Testamentum*, July 1978, XXVIII, Fasc. 3, pp. 336-48.

[13] Von Rad, *op. cit.*, p. 48.

[14] Walter Zimmerli, *I Mose 1-11, Die Urgeschichte*, Zürich: Zwingli, 1943, p. 54 (trans. from the German).

XII   A FIERY MASS

During the research for this volume I discovered once again to my joy that the Bible is capable of providing the believer with as much revelation as he is able to receive. The Spirit of God continued to reveal as I pored over dozens of commentaries.

There are scriptural hints — reasonable indications — concerning the condition of "Earth" *prior to* Gen. 1. These clues appear, not in scriptures that look back to the Creation, but rather are found in passages that refer ahead to the fiery judgment.

Tohu wabohu, the Hebrew words of Gen. 1:2, are typically translated "formless and void" or "a formless void." The usual interpretation of verse 2 implies a chaotic condition, but in Isaiah and Jeremiah those two words describe — in context — a condition typified by destruction, heat, fire and/or smoke. While *tohu* is occasionally found alone, *tohu wabohu* are used together only these two additional times.

> Her streams shall be turned into pitch,
>   and her soil into brimstone;
>   her land shall become burning pitch.
> Night and day it shall not be quenched;
>   its smoke shall go up forever.
> From generation to generation it shall lie waste;
>   none shall pass through it for ever and ever.
> ...He shall stretch the line of *tohu* over it,
>   and the plummet of *bohu*. (Isaiah 34:9-11)

"The picture is that of a ruined city surrounded by a land on fire, whose 'smoke shall go up forever.'"[1]

---

[1] R. B. Y. Scott, "Isaiah," *The Interpreter's Bible*, Vol. 5, Nashville:

Then "Jeremiah compose[d] a little poem on the subject
'a vision of cosmic destruction.' ...His poetic eye sees...the
invasion of chaos itself, as though the earth were returned to
its primeval condition of 'waste and void' — the *tohu wabohu*
that prevailed before the creation..."[2]

> I looked on the earth, and lo, it was *tohu wabohu*,
>   and to the heavens, and they had no light.
> I looked on the mountains, and lo, they were quaking,
>   and all the hills moved to and fro.
> ...I looked, and lo, the fruitful land was a desert,
>   and all its cities were laid in ruins
>   before the Lord, before his fierce anger.
> ...For this the earth shall mourn,
>   and the heavens above be black. (Jer. 4:23-28)

Both of these scriptures appear to be apocalyptic visions,
future catastrophic reversals of the creation pattern.[3]

Tohu wabohu together form a figure of speech known as
"hendiadys," in which two nouns connected by "and" actually
use one noun to qualify the other. An example would be,
"He approached with kindness and words," meaning, "He
approached with kind words," a construction rarely found in
English. Therefore *tohu wabohu* could hardly mean
"unformed and void," because one would have to modify the
other.[4] Gen. 1:2 and Jer. 4:23 are both examples of
hendiadys, but the two words are separated within the same
clause in Isaiah 34:11.

What does *tohu* mean? And what does *bohu* mean? And
what do the two words mean in hendiadys? Scholars are not
at all certain of the precise meaning of *tohu wabohu*.

Abingdon, 1952, p. 357.

[2] Anderson, *Creation versus Chaos, op. cit.*, p. 12.

[3] Fishbane, *op. cit.*, pp. 151-67.

[4] Speiser, *op. cit.*, p. 5.

Keil & Delitzsch note that its etymology is lost.[5]
Skinner adds, "The exact meaning...is difficult to make out."[6]
Ryle says the words are "untranslatable."[7] Franz Delitzsch
however suggests that these two Hebrew words

> ...go near to representing primitive matter as a fiery
> stream; the process of formation was indeed prepared
> for by the *tohu* being flooded over by the *tehom*...
> Darkness...settled over this flood of waters, in which
> the fervid heat of chaos was quenched.[8]

Here we discover a most interesting clue to the meaning of
these words. Perhaps *tohu wabohu* means just that — "a
fiery mass." The ancient Jewish rabbis perceived *tohu
wabohu* as being restricted deep within the earth during the
present age.[9] *Tohu wabohu* seemed to the rabbis to possess
almost a personality, and it strains impatiently at its bonds,
anticipating the Day of its release in judgment, much like
the "four angels who are bound at the great river Euphrates"
in Rev. 9:14. Even *tohu* used apart from *bohu* seems to
indicate more of heat or burning than our Hebrew lexicons
suggest, particularly as found in Deut. 32:10a; Job 6:18b; and
Isaiah 24:10a.

Consider a model based upon the exegesis. A "small,"
possibly-degenerate stellar mass is moving through the near-
emptiness of space. This preprimeval earth approaches a
smaller, *icy* body which reaches the Roche limit and

---

[5] C. F. Keil & F. Delitzsch, *Biblical Commentary on the Old
Testament,* Vol. I, trans. James Martin, Grand Rapids:
Eerdmans, 1951, p. 48.

[6] *Skinner, op. cit.,* p. 16.

[7] H. E. Ryle, *The Book of Genesis,* Cambridge: Cambridge Univ.
Press, 1914, p. 4.

[8] Delitzsch, *op. cit.,* pp. 80,81.

[9] Ginzberg, *op. cit.,* Vol. I, pp. 10,11.

disintegrates violently as the result of tidal stresses, much of the debris inundating the surface of fiery Earth with mountains of ice.[10] Most of the ice would have become steam prior to striking proto-Earth due to conversion of initial potential energy of separation into kinetic energy from its acceleration to Earth's fiery surface.[11]

The catastrophic nature of this encounter can be imagined; but the results are intriguing: the igneous earth retains its molten core (*tohu wabohu*); a thin layer of basement rock is congealed instantly by the shocking interaction of ice and magma; and a watery ocean of melted ice (*tehom*) covers the rock to a depth of hundreds or thousands of feet. Much of the moisture remains suspended in a steamy atmosphere adjacent to the surface.

There we find a most plausible model of proto-Earth to which Gen. 1:2 may well be referring. It is at this point, according to Gen. 1, that God becomes aggressively involved — verse 3, the first "Day" of Creation Week.

This model, incidentally, provides a most satisfying alternative explanation for Gentry's pleochroic halos in pre-Cambrian bedrock. Massive torrents of ice, water and vapor would have hardened the surface magma to create Earth's lithosphere quite suddenly.

This cosmic deluge of ice could be described as an event *preceding* the Creation of Gen. 1 or possibly implied in verse 2 as the initial creative act of Day One. Psalms 104:6 may be confirming just such an interpretation: "Thou didst cover [the earth] with [*tehom*] as with a garment..." If this verse is referring to the

---

[10] Patten, *op. cit.*, p. 161, hints at such a cosmogony.

[11] Apparently this phenomenon of scalding rain occurred again later, during the Flood, as was noted in Chapter I (Ginzberg, *op. cit.*, Vol. I, p. 159).

Creation (as many feel it is), then the inundation of *tohu wabohu* by *tehom* would indeed have been God's first creative act on behalf of the earth; Day One would have included two distinct works, as did Days Three and Six. Vail notes the Roman myth of the

> ...titanic contest between the powers of Vulcan and Neptune. How the waters on high descended, while yet the earth was a hot and seething mass, and were again and again flung into space by the irritated fires; till, finally, worried by the eternal attacks of Neptune, the fires grew tame, and the oceans of vapor settled upon the earth.[12]

Again we find a mythological distortion of the true record available to the ancient world, where in this case fire and water were considered by the Romans to be controlled by, and were themselves, gods. The sons of Noah knew the true story, but their increasingly paganized descendants gradually "re-mythologized" the memory. 17th and 18th century scientists disputed among themselves concerning whether primeval Earth was molten or watery. *Tohu wabohu* and *tehom* suggest that both were correct. At any rate, the waters have already inundated the fiery chaos prior to Gen. 1:3, the proclamation of light.

The icy visitor's demise adjacent to the molten earth, so clearly portrayed in ancient mythology, would thus have provided the "raw material" for the waters that were separated on Day Two. The near atmosphere of the earth must surely have been a vast steam bath until in Gen. 1:7 God lifted the intense moisture — probably by natural means — into the higher atmosphere to form *mabbul*, the antediluvian vapor canopy. Our waterless planet may have received its entire water supply[13] in two stages — all of it originating from

---

12 Vail, *op. cit.*, p. 14.

13 According to Champ Clark (*Flood*, Alexandria, VA: Time-Life Books, 1982, p. 24), Earth's current total quantity of water is 326,000,000 cubic miles.

this proposed initial cosmic intruder — first, in the Creation and, second, in the Flood as *mabbul* was condensed to fall as rain.

Patten however has similarly proposed an icy model for the later Deluge and its attendant Ice Epoch.[14] If his model for the Flood is correct, Earth could have received its hydrosphere from two separate bodies of ice shattering centuries apart. Patten estimates the rise in ocean levels during the Ice Age/Deluge to have totalled 12,000,000 to 14,000,000 cubic miles of water, with a significant amount of this water having been already in the atmosphere in the form of the vapor canopy (from the earlier ice dump at the Creation). Dillow[15] estimates the vapor canopy to have contained 6.219×10^{21} cubic centimeters of precipitable water, thus (if Dillow's estimate is correct) reducing the necessary size of Patten's proposed invading ice mass by nearly 1,500,000 cubic miles of available water (ice).

Perhaps the suddenness of the "attack" upon fiery proto-Earth by this pre-creation icy body could also suggest an explanation for the presence of iron and other heavy metals in the earth's crust rather than in the core alone. Of further interest, most deposits of iron ore for commercial mining are found between 45 and 65 degrees north latitude. Could the proposed explosive violence to our molten planet explain those anomalies?

The igneous nature of proto-Earth would conform to what has been similarly learned in recent years about the composition and "high" temperatures of Venus and the four Jovian planets. This primeval planet too would have been giving off excess heat, as most of its neighbors in the Solar System continue to emit to this day.

---

[14] Patten, *op. cit.*, pp. 143f.

[15] Dillow, *op. cit.*, p. 268.

As God once appropriated his privilege of returning planet Earth to its earlier *watery* condition during the Flood, so He will some day seize that privilege again to restore his creation to its primal, *fiery* pre-existence. At this point 1 Cor. 3:13; 2 Peter 3:7,10; and Rev. 8f provide quite graphic reading. As *tehom* tries repeatedly to overflow the earth in its diurnal tides and is muzzled by Earth's Sustainer, so too *tohu wabohu* continually strains to break its bonds through vulcanism, but God's restraining power will not release the fire before its time. Amos 7:4 predicts that day of a "...judgment by fire, and it devoured the great deep [*tehom*]." At the prophet's plea, the Lord God suspended the judgment temporarily. "But by the same word the heavens and earth that now exist have been stored up for fire..." (2 Peter 3:7a). Revelation pictures too that final release of *tohu wabohu* which will indeed "devour" *tehom*, delivering the earth at last from its partial domination by the waters: "...and the sea was no more" (Rev. 21:1c). In mythological terms, as Neptune once tamed Vulcan, so Vulcan will have the final victory. Does *tohu wabohu* obtain its revenge against *tehom*?

Thus the following is suggested as an alternative translation of Gen. 1:2: "...the earth being [or possibly, having been] *a fiery mass* and darkness being upon the face of the deep and the Spirit of God moving over the face of the waters..." Certainly this proposal deserves further investigation.

The very reasonable model proposed as a direct result of the exegesis — conforming remarkably to the natural evidence provided by the earth and its nearest neighbors — is another indication of the *revelatory* nature of the Bible. No man could have seen what is described, yet the narrative exhibits a startling aura of accuracy. How utterly fascinating to study Earth's natural history and discover that God's word described it first!

XIII A CREATION MODEL

God is consistent. "I the Lord do not change" (Mal. 3:6a). "Jesus Christ is the same yesterday and today and for ever" (Heb. 13:8). God operates within his own established laws. The limitations of the First Law of Thermodynamics (conservation of energy) as well as the Second Law (entropy) are apparent throughout scripture. However, the interruptions of those natural laws that occurred during Creation Week are also found to be in accordance with God's laws — such interruptions have occurred repeatedly since — during the Exodus, in the ministries of the Old Testament prophets, of Jesus of Nazareth and of the Church to this day. God still accomplishes creative miracles; he has built miracles into the order of the universe. Jesus repeated most emphatically that faith brings them about. God's creative power continues to function — in the normal sustentative capacity but also in miraculous response to prayer and faith — in this modern world.

Such miracles are not destructive, catastrophic; they reverse the natural entropy. Creation Week was apparently a fascinating combination of the catastrophic and the creative, both of which God used for his purposes. All but one of the five acts of Creation's first four days appear to have been catastrophic, "natural" events, causing major convulsions in the heavens and on the earth. The remaining two days were composed totally of three creative, life-giving acts.

Although creative miracles are a normative quality of God's working in this earth, worldwide catastrophes are quite intrusive (even if they have been ordered by God). The

169

creative miracles are supernatural, but the catastrophes are natural, the precise *timing* and *placing* of the latter events designating God's miraculous intervention. A correct perception of these cataclysmic miracles is a necessity for understanding parts of the Bible. Two contrasting examples will suffice. The multiplication of food for Elijah and the widow in 1 Kings 17 was a creative miracle; the damming of the Jordan River in Joshua 3 was the result of a local catastrophe, miraculous specifically in its exact timing and location. The catastrophic miracles of Gen. 1 involved the inanimate world: the establishing of light, the vapor canopy, the dry land and the heavenly bodies. The creative miracles provided life: vegetation, the various orders of the animal kingdom and, finally, man himself. "In him was life..." (John 1:4a).

Further, as the exegesis has already established, these catastrophes must have been cosmic, involving more than Earth alone. Terrestrial forces are far too insignificant to have caused a Deluge, an Ice Age, a separation of the continents, an apparent slowing of the earth's rotation (Joshua 10), an apparent slight backward motion of the rotating earth (2 Kings 20:11),[1] as well as the future onslaught seen in Revelation. Earthbound forces — primeval or present — could not possibly have caused "all the fountains of the great deep" to erupt almost simultaneously. From the world of modern science similar questions are raised by K. Krauskopf:

> "What are the irresistible forces which can twist and break the strongest rocks?" "Where do the forces originate which can raise and lower continental masses vertically?" "Why have not forces in the crust long

---

[1] The "long day" and the later backward movement of the shadow on the sundial were probably the experienced effects of spin axis precessions caused by near-misses with passing celestial bodies See Patten, Hatch, Steinhauer, *op. cit.*, pp. 113-29.

since reached an equilibrium?" With questions like these we have long since reached an impasse.[2] Krauskopf asks compelling questions. We must find additional dynamics.

Since the Old Testament authors wrote from an earthbound perspective, cosmic events tended to be viewed rather provincially. Many catastrophes were pictured only from the standpoints of their local terrestrial effects; the celestial upheavals often passed unmentioned. The earlier chapter, "The Waters," demonstrated however that the entire cosmos was understood by the ancient author to have been implicated in the Deluge. "The heavens and the earth" were all involved implicitly in the narrations of the various catastrophes, although not always noted explicitly. Certainly the future dissolution by fire is cosmic: "...the heavens will be kindled and dissolved..." (2 Peter 3:12b).

Thus a reasonable geogeny must posit natural factors that are not specifically mentioned in the Bible. These factors were all *extra-terrestrial*: they provided the dynamics needed to accomplish the catastrophes that God commanded in Gen. 1 and the subsequent massive changes that have occurred to that creation. One or more icy bodies have already been proposed. For explicit descriptions (albeit couched in mythological language), we look also to the vast body of ancient literature. And it is replete with countless sources of information concerning historical catastrophes, with remarkable confirmations of each other in widely separated cultures. Tragically, modern science chooses to ignore these informative records.

Is the universe stable? Patten *et al.* propose a series of

---

[2] Allan O. Kelly and Frank Dachille, *Target: Earth, The Role of Large Meteors in Earth Science*, Carlsbad, CA: 1953, p. 76, quoted in Alfred de Grazia, *The Lately Tortured Earth*, Princeton: Metron Publications, 1983, p. 282.

cosmic catastrophes, all of them noted in the Old Testament.[3]

> If one accepts the notion of uniformitarianism, one must be prepared to defend the concept of a serene solar system, placid for at least the last 500,000,000 years. It is our contention that the concept of a serene solar system cannot be defended at all; it cannot be defended for the last 5,000 years (much less for the last 500,000,000 years).[4]

However, any assumptions of historical global catastrophes must undergo two critical tests. (1) They must conform to the evidences of such enormous events as depicted in the literatures of various ancient cultures, and (2) they must be able to survive all scientific attempts to falsify them. Otherwise the proposed processes are to be abandoned or, more optimistically, emended until they can finally endure such rigorous examination. If the literary and/or scientific data were to succeed in disproving the idea of specific, historical, cosmic catastrophes, such proposals would thus be demonstrated to be mere *ad hoc* explanations, of no more value than the concordistic theories mentioned earlier. The reader is encouraged to refute all or part of this model of God's creation from each discipline — biblical, historical and mythological, and the pertinent scientific disciplines — without resort to post-Enlightenment categories of thought. Surely errors are to be found in this book, but those errors should cause no one to "throw the baby out with the bath water."

The planets of the Solar System possess a great deal of

---

[3] Thomas Burnet, in *The Sacred History of the Earth* (1690), proposed that the Flood might have been caused by the near passage of a comet (Brewster, *op. cit.*, p. 130); William Whiston, in his *New Theory of the Earth* (1696), suggested the same. The comet theory is once again finding respectability in scientific circles during the present generation.

[4] Patten, *op. cit.*, p. 26.

angular momentum — very much unequally distributed — a fact which seems to indicate cosmic catastrophes in the past. A violent history is clearly suggested by a number of additional conditions, such as the moon craters, the asteroids, Venus' retrograde rotation, the battered surface and dry river beds of Mars (a planet that never had an ocean or an atmosphere), Saturn's rings and Pluto's anomalous orbit. Earth's mid-Atlantic rift, the Great Rift Valley in the eastern hemisphere, the violently-buried fossils in sedimentary strata, and orogeny in general, provide ample evidences of cosmic catastrophes directly affecting our planet. Many additional silent witnesses could be noted. These enormous scars, some of them quite recent,[5] speak forcefully of natural disasters which the Bible says simply were ordained by God. Again, earthbound forces are utterly insufficient; therefore extraterrestrial factors must have been the servants of the Lord.

Even evolutionary paleontologists are today increasingly looking to the skies for the causes of what they perceive to be sudden, mass extinctions of life in the past, in particular, the abrupt, global termination of what has been arbitrarily termed the Cretaceous Period. They are beginning to realize that the simultaneity of massive catastrophes worldwide requires extraterrestrial agents. How slowly, how painfully is modern science inching toward the truth concerning Earth's

---

[5] Patten, Hatch and Steinhauer (*op. cit.*, pp. 259-60) suggest that a widening of the Great Rift Valley, from Israel to Southern Africa, occurred during the Sodom and Gomorrah holocaust as depicted in Gen. 19. De Grazia, in *Chaos and Creation* (*op. cit.*, p. 166), describes the memory of adjacent peoples of the horrors surrounding this geologic event in not-so-ancient history. The "division" of the earth (Gen. 10:25) is also recent, North America apparently breaking off from Europe and South America from Africa. The Americas' joining at Panama is even more recent, attested by the fact that the fauna and flora are quite different north and south of the Isthmus.

cataclysmic history!

Earlier there was proposed a model for the initial catastrophe involving the earth, a cosmic "accident" in which this molten proto-planet was "attacked" by ice, congealing the earth's basement rock and adding its hydrosphere. Thus was provided the raw material for God's Creation.

Day One brought the creation of light. The earth was apparently already rotating in order to provide the daily alternation of light and darkness. All events in Gen. 1 are viewed as from the earth.

> The most advanced astronomer of our day will speak of the sunrise and the sunset and of sending *up* a rocket. Such language is geocentric, but it is not in error. Genesis one...does not claim that the earth is the physical center of the universe.[6]

The source of that light on Day One? 2nd and 1st millennium B.C. Hebrews, not having been schooled in uniformitarianism and rationalistic philosophies, would have been untroubled by the light appearing three days before the sun found its permanent place.[7] Scripture does not answer this question.

Although God is light (1 John 1:5), the light of Day One did not emanate from Him. Here is the most obvious difference between Genesis and pagan cosmogonies where a god (or, gods) not only controls but is also identified with the substance out of which matter is created. The Creator of the universe is not a part of nature; He *commands* the various components, all of which are totally material and subservient to the unique God who is Spirit.

So we are led by the "light question" to skip ahead briefly to Day Four, when "God made the two lights...; he made the stars also." These verses describe a putting into their proper

---

[6] E. J. Young, *op. cit.*, p. 93; cf. *ibid.* p. 32; Leupold, *op. cit.*, p. 45.

[7] Ginzberg, Vol. I, *op. cit.*, pp. 8,9.

places of "the greater light" and "the lesser light." Neither the sun nor the moon is specifically named.

Strangely, the world's most ancient pagan cosmogonies insist that "the lesser light to rule the night" was none other than what we today call *Saturn*! And in times recent enough to be remembered and recorded by our forefathers! Such a suggestion would seem preposterous if the tradition were not so widespread. Ancient sources worldwide — from Egypt to Mesopotamia to India to China to Mexico — universally recall an antediluvian "Golden Age" when Saturn (the gas giant which may be the dark remains of a star) prominently ruled the night skies. Saturn's ancient Greek name, Chronos, still connotes the measurement of time: "...and let them be for signs and for seasons and for days and years..." (Gen. 1:14b). An incredibly violent *cosmic* upheaval must have occurred, perhaps provoking the Flood (and the Ice Age) and restructuring the greater part of the Solar System. Mythological records worldwide confirm one another in this statement. Our moon may be an astronomical "newcomer." Just what did occur has been the subject of investigations by many modern scholars.[8]

Why should Christians have difficulty with such a

---

[8] See, e.g., Cardona, "Let There Be Light," *Kronos*, Vol. III, 3, pp. 34-55; Velikovsky, "On Saturn and the Flood," *ibid.*, Vol. V, No. 1, pp. 3f; David N. Talbott, *The Saturn Myth*, Garden City, N.Y.: Doubleday, 1980; de Grazia, *Chaos and Creation, op. cit.*, pp. 179f; Giorgio de Santillana & Hertha von Dechend, *Hamlet's Mill: An Essay on Myth and the Frame of Time*, Boston: Gambit, 1969; Patten, *op. cit.*, pp. 309f.

The ancient rabbis apparently agreed: Cf. Velikovsky, "Khima and Kesil," *Kronos*, Vol. III, No. 4, 1978, p. 23, where he translates the Jewish Talmud (Tractate Brakhot, Fol. 59), "Two stars erupted from the planet Saturn and caused the Deluge." Incidentally, Saturn and some of its satellites are all or partially composed of water.

proposed upheaval in the recent history of the Solar System? Catastrophic history according to the Bible is not merely earthbound but totally cosmic, as pointed out earlier. Repeatedly the scriptures promise a not-too-distant future demise of the sun, e.g., Isaiah 13:10; 24:23; 34:4; Ezek. 32:7; Joel 2:10,31; 3:15; Amos 5:20; 8:9; Zeph. 1:15; Matt. 24:29; Mark 13:24; 2 Peter 3:10; Rev. 6:12; 8:12; 16:8; 21:23; 22:5. If we believe in such a *future* astronomical catastrophe, our world view should allow for similar disasters recorded in the Old Testament era. Is it not true that even Christians who study origins are also deeply affected by uniformitarian thinking?

So, although the Bible does not speak directly of Saturn's former nighttime prominence as do many other ancient records, still the unnamed "lesser light" of Gen. 1:16 clearly allows for this possibility. Whatever took place at the word of God on Day Four necessarily entails some speculation. However, the exegesis maintains that Day Four was the *ordering* of the Solar System (and perhaps beyond) *in relation to the earth.* The source of Earth's light on Day One remains a matter for speculation with so little data available, although there will one day be "no need of sun or moon to shine upon it, for the glory of God is its light, and its lamp is the Lamb" (Rev. 21:23). Day One, Day Four.

The earth after that first day was a steaming chaos. So God separated the waters above the earth from the ocean waters below to institute the vapor canopy, perhaps a temperature inversion high above the earth.[9] The mechanism God utilized for this remarkable "separation" would make an interesting study. Perhaps Earth's primeval heat alone would have been sufficient to establish the canopy. A rather

---

[9] See Dillow, *op. cit.*, for an examination of the varieties of possible vapor or ice canopies.

uniformly warm, moist climate enveloped the earth; air pressure was perhaps two or three times what it is today;[10] but the surface was still all *tehom*, the rebellious ocean waters. Day Two.

Another catastrophe occurred on Day Three. "God said, 'Let the waters under the heavens be gathered together into one place, and let the dry land appear.' And it was so." Again it is suggested that God brought a *larger* cosmic body close to the geoidal earth, the resulting tidal forces — this time on the earth — causing a massive upheaval in the crust to expose a single land mass, Pangaea. Would two interplanetary bodies engaging the earth within what may have been a brief time seem far-fetched? Not if the first (the icy one) were a mere satellite of a much larger mass that later passed near the earth on Day Three. In fact, Patten proposes just such a two-body invasion as the cause of the Deluge centuries later, a catastrophic event actually recorded in every ancient mythology.[11] Violent tidal convulsions of both hydrosphere and lithosphere were the order of the day, Day Three.

Thus is pictured a catastrophic sequence for the first four days of the Creation. Including Day Three's creation of the plant kingdom, the remainder of God's acts were all creative miracles.

Surely some inspired speculation could suggest additional possibilities. Perhaps the largely molten proto-Earth, only recently relieved of its fiery surface, might account in part for the universal "warmth" of the antediluvian period.[12]

---

[10] *Ibid.*, p. 233.

[11] Patten, *op. cit.*, p. 137f.

[12] The 18th century Comte de Buffon attempted to date the earth's age by how rapidly its interior was cooling from a presumed once-molten state; cf. Hallam, *op. cit.*, p. 82. This technique figured largely in similar subsequent attempts until the continental drift, or plate tectonics theory began gaining acceptance in very recent years.

Earth's molten core surely would have included more of what is today the thick (1800 miles), plastic mantle beneath the very thin lithosphere. We need not place the full burden of the Paleozoic calefaction on the "greenhouse" effect alone. A slowly cooling earth could perhaps contribute to the long-range instability of Dillow's model of a temperature inversion. Sooner or later his proposed vapor canopy had to collapse.[13]

Certainly all the discrepancies between biblical and modern chronologies have not been resolved here, but only the age of *inorganic* Earth. The dating of the creative results of Days Five and Six — *hayah nephesh*, "life itself" — will still remain embroiled in controversy. I have spoken primarily to the former, and much less to the origins of life upon the earth. Although the point is not central to this study, I also remain convinced that, in agreement with scripture, life is quite young in geological terms. And I continue to maintain that there need be no conflict between theology and geology; Gen. 1 makes good sense *and* good science!

The Drama of Creation then may be described as God's *ordering*, much as a designer "creates" the interior of a home by selecting and arranging the various pieces of furniture and accessories. "God *set* them in the firmament of the heavens..." (Gen. 1:17).

Apparently He chose selectively from the universe, bringing together disparate components to "furnish" his "house." Previous theories of planetary origins seem to be ruled out by their great variety: their diverse composition, varied orbits, angular momentum, temperatures and size, retrograde rotation, strongly tilted axes, and other incongruous characteristics. God gathered together (in what we today would term catastrophes) wandering, dissonant

---

[13] Dillow, *op. cit.*, pp. 263f.

participants, impressing them into his own symphony, and allowed the descendants of Adam to title it the Solar System.

"Thus the heavens and the earth were finished, and all the host of them" (Gen. 2:1).

XIV   CONCLUSION

In summary, I have sought to demonstrate a number
of points.

(1) Scriptural exegesis reveals that the Bible does not
speak of *creatio ex nihilo*, but tells of a creation
out of existing material — material which stubbornly resisted God's creativity.

(2) This exegesis provides the only interpretation of
Gen. 1:1-3 that is not self-contradicting. It
confirms itself throughout the Bible.

(3) We have traced historically the heretical origins of
creatio ex nihilo and its subsequent, almost-but-
never-complete adoption by the Christian Church.

(4) Creation out of nothing should now be removed
from scientific creationism's biblical expositions.

(5) The creation narrative of Gen. 1 need not be
demythologized; it had already been demythologized when first written. The chapter is historical,
in deliberate chronological order.

(6) What has hitherto appeared to be a most awkward
— even mythological — order of the events of
creation in Gen. 1 now seems more plausible
scientifically.

(7) Some commentators permit a chronology Gen. 1
does not demand, while others demand a chronology Gen. 1 does not permit.

(8) The chronology presented in Gen. 1 allows for
certain old earth indicators and certain young
earth indicators, contributing toward a resolution
of creationists' disagreement over our planet's age.

(9) Concordistic theories are not only invalid; they are unnecessary. Scientific creationists should not compromise with the pagan culture about us by accepting *scientistic* dogma that varies with each generation.

(10) Contrary to much creationist literature, the natural and supernatural laws in effect during Creation Week are indeed the same laws which are quite operative to this day.

(11) A valid creation model can be drawn from a detailed study of relevant scriptures in conjunction with other appropriate disciplines.

(12) By the inclusion of this book's insights, scientific creationism will be more systematic and logical.

(13) The Bible and modern science can truthfully speak in agreement.

(14) Creation science should now be making a more significant contribution to our perception of the overall unity of the Bible and God's working in history.

(15) Our Creator is highly exalted, yet remains ever-so-much involved in our lives.

Creationists should courageously re-examine Earth's age indicators in the light of scripture. My hope is that this book will strengthen a Christian's trust in the inerrancy of the Bible and of the great God who in it revealed his very personal story of the Creation. "...I the LORD your God am a jealous [read, passionate] God..." (Exodus 20:5b). I have attempted to accomplish this goal simply by allowing the Hebrew text to speak on its own (non-modern) terms. A literalistic acceptance of the historical and revelatory portions of scripture — in their ancient contexts — is for me the only valid way to understand them.

I have been greatly encouraged in this study by the discovery that, for the first time in more than a millennium, evangelical scholars are today finding for themselves, as I have, the impossibility of *ex nihilo* creation in Gen. 1. Realizing too that some readers may be partially or totally unconvinced, I present this thesis to the Christian world for its heuristic value, trusting that it will stimulate further discussion, research, and surely, prayer. I trust too that open-minded creationists will expose this presentation to the process of falsification. Most of the material presented is of a non-scientific nature, so it is hoped that interested scientists who are creationists will pursue the various questions and suggestions raised.

There are yet many unanswered questions, but the reader may take comfort in knowing that those Christian commentators who claim competing concepts of creation confront a more clamorous covey of cacophonous contradictions.

APPENDIX

Following are fifteen modern translations of Gen. 1:1-3 which vary from the Septuagint tradition. The first five are modelled after Rashi's interpretation, the remainder copy Ibn Ezra.

(1) In the beginning when God created the heavens and the earth, and while the earth was still unformed and chaotic, with darkness on the surface of the deep, and the Spirit of God brooding over the waters, God said, "Let there be light," and there was light." (Charles F. Kent, *The Old Testament*, 1921).

(2) When God began to create heaven and earth — and the earth was chaotic and empty, and darkness was over the primordial ocean, and the spirit of God was hovering over the water —, (then) God said, Let light come into existence, and light came into existence. (William F. Albright, "Contributions to Biblical Archaeology and Philology, *Journal of Biblical Literature*, Vol. 43, 1924)

(3) When God began to create the heaven and the earth — the earth being unformed and void, with darkness over the surface of the deep and a wind from God sweeping over the water — God said, "Let there be light"; and there was light. (Jewish Publication Society of America, *The Torah*, 1962)

(4) When God began to create the heavens and the earth, the earth having been without form and void, darkness being upon the face of the deep and the spirit of God soaring over the face of the waters, God said, "Let there be light"; and there was light. (W. R. Lane, "The Initiation of Creation," *Vetus Testamentum*, Vol. XIII, 1963, p. 72).

(5) When God set about to create heaven and earth — the world being then a formless waste, with

darkness over the seas and only an awesome wind sweeping over the water — God said, "Let there be light." And there was light. (E. A. Speiser, *The Anchor Bible*, 1964).

(6) In the beginning of God's preparing the heavens and the earth — the earth hath existed waste and void, and darkness is on the face of the deep, and the Spirit of God fluttering on the face of the waters, and God saith, "Let light be"; and light is. (Robert Young, *Young's Literal Translation*, 1887)

(7) When God began to form the universe, the world was void and vacant, darkness lay over the abyss; but the Spirit of God was hovering over the waters, God said, "Let there be light," and there was light. (James Moffatt, *A New Translation of the Bible*, 1922)

(8) When God began to create the heavens and the earth, the earth was a desolate waste, with darkness covering the abyss and a tempestuous wind raging over the surface of the waters. Then God said, "Let there be light!" And there was light. (J. M. P. Smith & Edgar Goodspeed, *An American Translation*, 1931)

(9) When God began to create the heavens and the earth, the earth was without form and void, and darkness was upon the face of the deep; and the Spirit of God was moving over the face of the waters. And God said, "Let there be light!"; and there was light. (*Revised Standard Version* [footnote], 1952)

(10) In the beginning of creation, when God made heaven and earth, the earth was without form and void, with darkness over the face of the abyss, and a mighty wind that swept over the surface of the waters. God said, "Let there be light," and there was light. (*New English Bible*, 1961)

(11) When God began to order heaven and earth, the earth was chaotic with darkness on the face of the Deep and with the Spirit of God flying over the surface of the waters; and [then] God said: "Let there be light!" and so there was light. (Cyrus H. Gordon, *Biblical Motifs: Origins and Transformations*, 1966)

(12) In the beginning, when God created the heavens and the earth, the earth was a formless wasteland, and darkness covered the abyss, while a mighty wind swept over the waters. Then God said, "Let there be light," and there was light. (*New American Bible*, 1970)

(13) When God began creating the heavens and the earth, the earth was at first a shapeless, chaotic mass, with the Spirit of God brooding over the dark vapors. Then God said, "Let there be light." And light appeared. (*The Living Bible*, 1971)

(14) In the beginning, when God created the universe, the earth was formless and desolate. The raging ocean that covered everything was engulfed in total darkness, and the power of God was moving over the water. Then God commanded, "Let there be light" — and light appeared. (*The Bible in Today's English Version*, 1976)

(15) In the beginning when Elohim had created the heavens and the earth, the earth was formless and waste; and darkness lay upon the face of the deep, and the spirit of Elohim brooded over the waters. (Harold G. Stigers, *A Commentary on Genesis*, 1976)

BIBLIOGRAPHY

G. Ch. Aalders, *Genesis*, Bible Student's Commentary, Vol. I, trans. William Heynen, Grand Rapids: Zondervan, 1981.

Oswald T. Allis, *God Spake by Moses*, Nutley, NJ: Presbyterian & Reformed Publishing Co., 1976.

Bernhard W. Anderson, *Creation versus Chaos*, New York: Association Press, 1967.

Ante-Nicene Fathers, Vol. I, Irenaeus, "Against Heresies"; Vol. III, Tertullian, "Against Hermogenes"; Vol. VII, Constitutions of the Holy Apostles"; Hippolytus, "The Refutation of All Heresies"; ed. Alexander Roberts & James Donaldson, Buffalo: Christian Literature Publishing Co., 1885.

The Apostolic Fathers, Vol. 6, "The Shepherd of Hermas," trans. Graydon F. Snyder, Camden: Thomas Nelson, 1968.

Donald Grey Barnhouse, *The Invisible War*, Grand Rapids: Zondervan, 1965.

Karl Barth, *Church Dogmatics*, Vol. III, part I, Edinburgh: T. & T. Clark, 1958.

W. I. B. Beveridge, *The Art of Scientific Investigation*, London: Heinemann, 1950.

Henri Blocher, *In the Beginning*, trans. David G. Preston, Downers Grove, IL: Inter-Varsity Press, 1984.

Thorlief Boman, *Hebrew Thought Compared with Greek*, Philadelphia: Westminster Press, 1960.

Edwin Tenney Brewster, *Creation: A History of Non-Evolutionary Theories*, Indianapolis: Bobbs-Merrill, 1927.

H. A. Brongers, *De Scheppingstradities bij de Profeten*, Amsterdam: H. J. Paris, 1945.

Francis Brown, S. R. Driver and Charles A. Briggs, *A Hebrew and English Lexicon of the Old Testament,* Oxford: The Clarendon Press, 1907 (reprinted 1959).

Walter Brueggemann, *Genesis,* Atlanta: John Knox Press, 1982.

Thomas Burnet, *The Sacred Theory of the Earth,* 1690.

John Calvin, *Commentaries on the Book of Genesis,* Vol. I, trans. John King, Grand Rapids: Eerdmans, 1948.

Umberto Cassuto, *A Commentary on the Book of Genesis,* trans. Israel Abrahams, Jerusalem: Magnes Press, 1944.

R. H. Charles, ed. *Pseudepigrapha,* Oxford: Clarendon Press, 1913.

James H. Charlesworth, *The Old Testament Pseudepigrapha,* 2 vols., Garden City, NY: Doubleday, 1983.

Brevard S. Childs, *Myth and Reality in the Old Testament,* Naperville, IL: Alec R. Allenson, 1960.

Champ Clark, *Planet Earth: Flood,* Alexandria, VA: Time-Life Books, 1982.

A. Cohen, *The Soncino Chumash,* Hindhead, Surrey: Soncino Press, 1947.

R. O. Corvin, *Home Bible Study Course,* Vols. I, V, Charlotte: PTL Club, 1976.

Peter C. Craigie, *Psalms 1-50,* Word Biblical Commentary, Waco: Word Books, 1983.

Mitchell Dahood, *Psalms I, Psalms II, Psalms III,* Anchor Bible, Garden City, NY: Doubleday, 1966.

Robert Davidson, *Genesis 1-11,* London: Cambridge Univ. Press, 1973.

Alfred de Grazia, *Chaos and Creation*, Princeton: Metron Publications, 1981.

_____, *Homo Schizo I*, Princeton: Metron Publications, 1983.

_____, *The Lately Tortured Earth*, Princeton: Metron Publications, 1983.

Franz Delitzsch, *A New Commentary on Genesis,* Edinburgh: T. & T. Clark, 1888.

Giorgio de Santillana & Hertha von Dechend, *Hamlet's Mill: An Essay on Myth and the Frame of Time,* Boston: Gambit, 1969.

Giorgio de Santillana, *The Crime of Galileo,* Chicago: Univ. of Chicago Press, 1955.

August Dillmann, *Genesis Critically and Exegetically Expounded,* trans. William B. Stevenson, Edinburgh: T. & T. Clark, 1897.

Joseph C. Dillow, *The Waters Above,* Chicago: Moody Press, 1981.

John Diodati, *Pious Annotations upon the Holy Bible*, London: Nicholas Fussell, 1543.

Marcus Dods, *The Book of Genesis*, Edinburgh: T. & T. Clark, 1911.

_____, *The Book of Genesis,* The Expositor's Bible, New York: A. C. Armstrong and Son, 1903.

S. R. Driver, *The Book of Genesis*, London: Methuen, 1904.

Walther Eichrodt, *Theology of the Old Testament*, trans. J. A. Baker, Philadelphia: Westminster, 1967.

Fridericus Field, *Origenis Hexaplorum supersunt,* Vol. I, Oxford: 1875.

Weston W. Fields, *Unformed and Unfilled*, Phillipsburg, NJ: Presbyterian & Reformed Publishing Co., 1978.

Jack Finegan, *In the Beginning*, New York: Harper & Bros., 1962.

Wilfrid Francis, *Coal: Its Formation and Composition*, 2nd ed., London: Edward Arnold, 1961.

Abraham Geiger, *Urschrift und Uebersetzungen der Bibel in ihrer Abhängigkeit von der innern Entwickelung des Judenthums*, 1857.

Langdon Gilkey, *Maker of Heaven and Earth*, Garden City, NY: Doubleday, 1959.

Louis Ginzberg, *The Legends of the Jews*, Vols. I & V, Philadelphia: The Jewish Publication Society of America, 1947.

Cyrus H. Gordon, *Ugaritic Textbook*, Rome: Pontifical Biblical Institute, 1965.

Robert Graves & Raphael Patai, *Hebrew Myths, The Book of Genesis*, Garden City, NY: Doubleday, 1964.

Hermann Gunkel, *Genesis*, 6th ed., Göttingen: Vanderhoeck & Ruprecht, 1964.

——————, *Schöpfung und Chaos in Urzeit und Endzeit*, Göttingen: Vanderhoeck & Ruprecht, 1895.

Robert Haardt, *Gnosis: Character and Testimony*, trans. J. F. Hendry, Leiden: E. J. Brill, 1971.

Francis C. Haber, *The Age of the World: Moses to Darwin*, Baltimore: The Johns Hopkins Press, 1959.

Anthony Hallam, *Great Geological Controversies*, Oxford & New York: Oxford Univ. Press, 1983.

William Hanna, *Posthumous Works of Thomas Chalmers*, Vol. I, New York: Harper, 1849.

James Hastings, *The Great Texts of the Bible*, Vol. I, New York: Charles Scribner's Sons, 1911.

Alexander Heidel, *The Babylonian Genesis*, 2nd ed., Chicago: Univ. of Chicago Press, 1951.

Karl Heim, *Christian Faith and Natural Science*, New York: Harper & Brothers, 1953.

Lancelot Hogben, *Mathematics for the Millions*, New York: W. W. Norton, 1937.

G. C. D. Howley, F. F. Bruce, H. L. Ellison, eds., *The New Layman's Bible Commentary*, Grand Rapids: Zondervan, 1979.

Conrad Hyers, *The Meaning of Creation*, Atlanta: John Knox Press, 1984.

Irenaeus, "Against Heresies," *Early Christian Fathers*, Vol. I, The Library of Christian Classics, Philadelphia: Westminster Press, 1953.

Edmond Jacob, *Theology of the Old Testament*, trans. Arthur W. Heathcote and Philip J. Allcock, London: Hodder & Stoughton, 1958.

The Book of Jasher, faithfully translated from the Original Hebrew into English, Salt Lake City: J. H. Parry & Co., 1887.

Jerome, *Letters*, LXIX, 6, in J.-P. Migne, *Patrologia Latina*, Vol. XXII, Paris: 1864.

C. F. Keil & F. Delitzsch, *Biblical Commentary on the Old Testament*, Vol. I, trans. James Martin, Grand Rapids: Eerdmans, 1951.

LeBaron W. Kinney, *Acres of Rubies*, New York: Loizeaux Brothers, 1942.

Rudolph Kittel, *Biblia Hebraica*, Stuttgart: Württembergische Bibelanstalt, 1937.

Eugene M. Klaaren, *Religious Origins of Modern Science,* Grand Rapids: Eerdmans, 1977.

Nathaniel Kravitz, *Genesis: A New Interpretation of the First Three Chapters,* New York: Philosophical Library, 1967.

H. C. Leupold, *Exposition of Genesis,* Grand Rapids: Baker, 1950.

O. Loretz, *Schöpfung und Mythos,* Stuttgart: 1968.

Lucretius, *On the Nature of Things,* Book I, 146, trans. H. A. J. Munro, *Great Books of the Western World,* Vol. 12, Chicago. Encyclopaedia Britannica, 1952.

Luther's Commentary on Genesis, Vol. I, trans. J. T. Mueller, Grand Rapids: Zondervan, 1958.

Michael Maher, *Genesis*, Wilmington, DE: Michael Glazier, 1982.

Moffatt, James, *The General Epistles,* The Moffatt New Testament Commentary, New York: Harper & Brothers, n.d.

James G. Murphy, *A Critical and Exegetical Commentary on the Book of Genesis,* Boston: Estes & Lauriat, 1873.

Origen, *Hexapla*, in J.-P. Migne, *Patrologiae Graecae*, Vol. XV, Paris: 1857.

Donald W. Patten, *The Biblical Flood and the Ice Epoch,* Seattle: Pacific Meridian, 1966.

_____, Ronald R. Hatch, Loren C. Steinhauer, *The Long Day of Joshua and Six Other Catastrophes,* Seattle: Pacific Meridian, 1973.

William Paul, *Analysis and Critical Interpretation of the Hebrew Text of the Book of Genesis*, Edinburgh & London: William Blackwood & Sons, 1852.

Arthur S. Peake, *A Commentary on the Bible,* London: T. C. & E. C. Jack, 1931.

John Pearson, *An Exposition of the Creed,* (first pub. 1659), rev. W. S. Dobson, New York: D. Appleton, 1844.

Johannes Pedersen, *Israel: Its Life and Culture,* 2 vols., London: Oxford Univ. Press, 1926.

G. H. Pember, *Earth's Earliest Ages,* New York: Fleming H. Revell, 1876.

J. B. Phillips, *Your God Is Too Small*, New York: Macmillan, 1953.

The Natural History of Pliny, Vol. I, trans. John Bostock and H. T. Riley, London: George Bell & Sons, 1893.

Marvin H. Pope, *Job,* Anchor Bible, Garden City, NY: Doubleday, 1965.

Ira M. Price, Ovid R. Sellers, E. Leslie Carson, *The Monuments and the Old Testament,* Philadelphia: The Judson Press, 1958.

Gilles Quispel, *Gnostic Studies,* I, Istanbul: Nederlands Instituut voor het Nabije Oosten, 1974.

Bernard Ramm, *The Christian View of Science and Scripture*, Grand Rapids: Eerdmans, 1955.

F. P. Ramsey, *An Interpretation of Genesis,* New York: Neale, 1911.

Rashi, *The Pentateuch and Rashi's Commentary, Genesis,* ed. Abraham ben Isaiah & Benjamin Sharfman, Brooklyn, NY: S. S. & R. Publishing Co., 1949.

N. H. Ridderbos, *Is There a Conflict Between Genesis 1 and Natural Science?* Grand Rapids: Eerdmans, 1957.

Jeremy Rifkin, with Ted Howard, *Entropy: a New World View,* New York: Viking Press, 1980.

H. E. Ryle, *The Book of Genesis,* Cambridge Bible for Schools & Colleges, Cambridge: Cambridge Univ. Press, 1914.

Nahum M. Sarna, *Understanding Genesis,* New York: McGraw-Hill, 1966.

John Skinner, *A Critical and Exegetical Commentary on Genesis,* International Critical Commentary, Edinburgh: T. & T. Clark, 1910.

William Smith & Henry Wace, eds., *A Dictionary of Christian Biography, Literature, Sects and Doctrines,* Vol. III, reprint of the 1877 edition, New York: AMS Press, 1974.

E. A. Speiser, *Genesis,* The Anchor Bible, Garden City, NY: Doubleday, 1964.

G. J. Spurrell, *Notes on the Hebrew Text of the Book of Genesis,* London: Methuen, 1904.

Harold G. Stigers, *A Commentary on Genesis,* Grand Rapids: Zondervan, 1976.

Arthur N. Strahler, *Physical Geology,* New York: Harper & Row, 1981.

David N. Talbott, *The Saturn Myth,* Garden City, NY: Doubleday, 1980.

Henry St. John Thackeray, *The Letter of Aristeas,* London: Society for the Promotion of Christian Knowledge, 1917.

Gene M. Tucker, *Form Criticism of the Old Testament,* Philadelphia: Fortress Press, 1971.

Merrill F. Unger, *Archaeology and the Old Testament,* Grand Rapids: Zondervan, 1954.

Isaac N. Vail, *The Earth's Annular System, or, The Waters above the Firmament*, 4th Edition, Pasadena: Annular World Co., 1912.

G. Van Groningen, *First Century Gnosticism*, Leiden: E. J. Brill, 1967.

Bruce Vawter, *A Path Through Genesis*, London: Sheed & Ward, 1957.

Immanuel Velikovsky, *Worlds in Collision*, New York: Doubleday, 1950.

_____ , *Earth in Upheaval*, New York: Doubleday, 1955.

Gerhard von Rad, *Genesis*, Philadelphia: Westminster, 1961.

Mary K. Wakeman, *God's Battle with the Monster*, Leiden: E. J. Brill, 1973.

Luther A. Weigle, *The Genesis Octapla*, New York: Thomas Nelson, 1952.

Herbert H. Wernecke, *The Book of Revelation Speaks to Us*, Philadelphia: Westminster Press, 1954.

Claus Westermann, *The Genesis Accounts of Creation*, trans. Norman E. Wagner, Philadelphia: Fortress Press, 1964.

William Whiston, *New Theory of the Earth*, 1696.

John C. Whitcomb, Jr. & Henry M. Morris, *The Genesis Flood*, Grand Rapids: Baker, reprint 1978.

Andrew Dickson White, *A History of the Warfare of Science with Theology in Christendom*, Vol. I, New York: D. Appleton & Co., 1898.

Davis A. Young, *Creation and the Flood*, Grand Rapids: Baker Book House, 1977.

_____ , *Christianity and the Age of the Earth*, Grand Rapids: Zondervan, 1982.

Edward J. Young, *Studies in Genesis One*, Phillipsburg, NJ: Presbyterian & Reformed Publishing Co., 1979.

Robert Young, *Concise Commentary on the Holy Bible*, Edinburgh: George Adam Young, 1904.

—————, *Young's Literal Translation of the Bible*, Revised Edition, Grand Rapids: Baker, 1956.

Walter Zimmerli, *I Mose 1-11, Die Urgeschichte*, Zürich: Zwingli, 1943.

Journal and Encyclopedia Articles

W. F. Albright, "Book Review of Alexander Heidel, *The Babylonian Genesis*," *Journal of Biblical Literature*, Vol. 62, 1943, pp. 366-70.

—————, "Contributions to Biblical Archaeology and Philology," *Journal of Biblical Literature*, Vol. 43, 1924, pp. 363-93.

—————, "The Old Testament and Archaeology," *Old Testament Commentary*, ed. Herbert C. Alleman & Elmer E. Flack, Philadelphia: Muhlenberg Press, 1948.

Bernhard W. Anderson, "Creation," *Interpreter's Dictionary of the Bible*, Vol. I, Nashville: Abingdon Press, 1962.

—————, "From Analysis to Synthesis: the Interpretation of Genesis 1-11," *Journal of Biblical Literature*, 97, 1978, pp. 23-39.

—————, "The Earth Is the Lord's," *Interpretation*, Vol. IX, 1955, pp. 3-20.

Bergman, Ringgren, Bernhardt, Botterweck, art. *"bara'*," *Theological Dictionary of the Old Testament*, Vol. II, ed. G. Johannes Botterweck & Helmer Ringgren, trans. John T. Willis, Grand Rapids: Eerdmans, 1975.

Jerry Bergman, "The Establishment of a Heliocentric View of the Universe," *Journal of the American Scientific Affiliation*, Vol. 33, No. 4, Dec. 1981, pp. 225-30.

Joshua Bloch, "The Influence of the Greek Bible on the Peshitta," *American Journal of Semitic Languages and Literatures*, XXXVI, January 1920, pp. 161-66.

Encyclopaedia Britannica, 15th ed., Vol. 1, art., "Arithmetic"; Vol. 11, art., "History of Mathematics."

Robert H. Brown, "Moses' Creation Account," *Ministry*, Sept. 1978.

Dwardu Cardona, "Let There Be Light," *Kronos*, Vol. III, No. 3, pp. 34-55; Vol. IV, No. 3, Forum: "Creation and Destruction," pp. 71-74.

Chemical and Engineering News, Oct. 11, 1976.

Brevard S. Childs, "The Enemy from the North and the Chaos Tradition," *Journal of Biblical Literature*, Vol. 78, 1959.

Christianity Today, Vol. XXVI, No. 16, October 8, 1982, editorials.

Mitchell J. Dahood, "Mišmār 'Muzzle' in Job 7:12," *Journal of Biblical Literature and Exegesis*, 80, 1961.

Gerhard Delling, art. in *Theological Dictionary of the New Testament*, Vol. 1, ed. Gerhard Kittel, trans. Geoffrey W. Bromiley, Grand Rapids: Eerdmans, 1964, pp. 452-54.

S. J. DeVries, "Chronology of the Old Testament," *Interpreter's Dictionary of the Bible*, Vol. I, Nashville: Abingdon Press, 1962.

Thomas Ferté, "A Record of Success," *Pensée*, Special Issue, Vol. II, No. 2, May 1972, pp. 11-15,23.

Michael Fishbane, "Jeremiah IV 23-26 and Job III 3-13: A Recovered Use of the Creation Pattern," *Vetus Testamentum*, Vol. XXI, 1971, pp. 151-167.

T. H. Gaster, "Cosmogony." *Interpreter's Dictionary of the Bible*, Vol. I, Nashville: Abingdon Press, 1962.

Cyrus H. Gordon, "Leviathan: Symbol of Evil," *Biblical Motifs: Origins and Transformations*, ed. Alexander Altmann, Cambridge: Harvard Univ. Press, 1966.

Alan H. Guth & Paul J. Steinhardt, "The Inflationary Universe," *Scientific American*, Vol. 250, No. 5, May 1984.

Gerhard F. Hasel, "Recent Translations of Genesis 1:1: A Critical Look," *The Bible Translator*, Vol. 22, No. 4, Oct. 1971, pp. 154-67.

D. Russell Humphreys, "The Creation of the Earth's Magnetic Field," *Creation Research Quarterly*, Vol. 20, No. 2, Sept. 1983.

Nicholas K. Kiessling, "Antecedents of the Medieval Dragon in Sacred History," *Journal of Biblical Literature*, LXXXIX, pp. 167-77.

David J. Krause, "Astronomical Distances, the Speed of Light, and the Age of the Universe," *Journal of the American Scientific Affiliation*, Vol. 33, No. 4, Dec. 1981.

W. R. Lane, "The Initiation of Creation," *Vetus Testamentum*, Vol. XIII, 1963, pp. 63-73.

Robert E. Lee, "Radiocarbon: Ages in Error," *Anthropological Journal of Canada*, Vol. 19, No. 3, 1981; reprinted in *Creation Research Society Quarterly*, Vol. 19, No. 2, Sept. 1982.

Conrad E. L'Heureux, "Understanding Old Testament Prophecies," *The Bible Today*, Vol. 23, No. 1, Jan. 1985, pp. 56-57.

Sean E. McEvenue, "The Narrative Style of the Priestly Writer," *Analecta Biblica*, 50, Rome: 1971.

Julian Morgenstern, "The Sources of the Creation Story," *American Journal of Semitic Languages and Literatures*, XXXVI, 1920, pp. 169-212.

William Overn, "The Creator's Signature," *Bible Science Newsletter*, Vol. 20, No. 1, Jan. 1982.

R. B. Y. Scott, "Isaiah," *The Interpreter's Bible*, Vol. 5, Nashville: Abingdon, 1952.

Barry Setterfield, "The Velocity of Light and the Age of the Universe," *Ex Nihilo*, Vol. 4, No. 1, March 1981, and Vol. 5, No. 3, Jan. 1983.

C. A. Simpson, "Genesis," *Interpreter's Bible*, Vol. I, Nashville: Abingdon, 1952.

J. M. Powis Smith, "The Syntax and Meaning of Genesis 1:1-3," *American Journal of Semitic Languages and Literatures*, 44, 1928, pp. 108-115.

Paul M. Steidl, "The Velocity of Light and the Age of the Universe," *Creation Research Society Quarterly*, Vol. 19, No. 2, Sept. 1982.

Carroll Stuhlmueller, "The Theology of Creation in Second Isaias," *Catholic Biblical Quarterly*, Vol. 21, 1959, pp. 429-67.

Merrill F. Unger, "Creation," *Unger's Bible Dictionary*, Chicago: Moody Press, 1957.

_____, "Rethinking the Genesis Account of Creation," *Bibliotheca Sacra*, Vol. 115, 1958, pp. 27-35.

Immanuel Velikovsky, "Khima and Kesil," *Kronos*, Vol. III, No. 4, 1978, pp. 19-23.

Howard Wallace, "Leviathan and the Beast in Revelation," *The Biblical Archaeologist*, Vol. XI, No. 3, pp. 61-68.

Bruce K. Waltke, "The Creation Account in Genesis 1:1-3," *Bibliotheca Sacra*, Parts 1-5, Jan. 1975 - Jan. 1976.

David C. C. Watson, "Dare We Reinterpret Genesis?" *Bible-Science Newsletter*, Vol. 22, No. 5, May 1984.

Gordon J. Wenham, "The Coherence of the Flood Narrative," *Vetus Testamentum*, July 1978, XXVIII, Fasc. 3, pp. 336-48.

Robert L. Whitelaw, "The Fountains of the Great Deep, and the Windows of Heaven," *Science at the Crossroads: Observation or Speculation?* Richfield, MN: Onesimus Publishing, 1985, pp. 95-104.

R. J. Wilson, "Wilhelm Vischer on 'God Created,'" *Expository Times*, LXV, 1953, pp. 94-95.

Wendy S. Wolbach, Roy S. Lewis, Edward Anders, "Cretaceous Extinctions: Evidence for Wildfires and Search for Meteoritic Material," *Science*, Vol. 230, No. 4722, Oct. 11, 1985, pp. 167-70.

Daniel Wonderly, "Non-Radiometric Data Relevant to the Question of Age," *Journal of the American Scientific Affiliation*, Vol. 27, No. 4, Dec. 1975.

"Monitor," *Workshop*, Vol. 6, No. 5, Society for Interdisciplinary Studies, February 1986.

Edward J. Young, "The Relation of the First Verse of Genesis One to Verses Two and Three," *Westminster Theological Journal*, Vol. XXI, No. 2, May 1959.

Heinrich Zimmern and T. K. Cheyne, art., "Creation," *Encyclopaedia Biblica*, Vol. I, ed. T. K. Cheyne and J. Sutherland Black, N.Y.: Macmillan, 1899.

SCRIPTURE INDEX

GENERAL INDEX